Hooray!
Let's Pray!

Group
Loveland, Colorado

Hooray! Let's Pray!

Credits
Editor: Lois Keffer
Creative Development Editor: Paul Woods
Chief Creative Officer: Joani Schultz
Copy Editor: Helen Turnbull
Art Director: Lisa Chandler
Assistant Art Director: Bill Fisher
Cover Art Director: Helen H. Lannis
Computer Graphic Artist: Kari K. Monson
Cover Designer: Liz Howe
Illustrator: Gary Templin
Production Manager: Ann Marie Gordon

Contributors
Jody Brolsma, Cindy Hansen, Lois Keffer, Jan Kershner, Barbie Murphy, Jackie Noll, Nancy Paulson, and Paul Woods

Library of Congress Cataloging-in-Publication Data
Hooray! let's pray / edited by Lois Keffer.
    p.   cm.
    ISBN 0-7644-2028-3
    1. Prayer--Christianity--Juvenile literature. 2. Christian education of children. I. Keffer, Lois.
    BV212.H66 1997
    268.432--dc21   97-10424
                                                               CIP
                                                               AC

10 9 8 7 6 5 4 3 2 1   06 05 04 03 02 01 00 99 98 97
Printed in the United States of America.

Hooray! Let's Pray! ● Hooray! Let's Pray! ● Hooray! Let's Pray!

Contents

● ● ● ● ● ● ● ● ● ● ● ● ● ● ● ● ● ● ● ●

Hooray! Let's Pray! ● Hooray! Let's Pray! ● Hooray! Let's Pray!

Isn't it incredible? God, the mighty Creator of the universe, invites us to two-way communication. Anytime. Anywhere. Are your kids excited about prayer, or has it become dull routine? Do they pray with enthusiasm, or is prayer time punctuated with fidgets and yawns?

Hooray! Let's Pray! is a treasure-trove of creative ideas that will have your kids looking forward to prayer time with eager anticipation. You'll find active prayers, quiet prayers, singing prayers, and all kinds of prayers for special times and places. The chapter entitled "Ready, Set, Pray!" offers active-learning ideas that will teach your kids important biblical principles about prayer. Another chapter tells how to pray effectively with preschoolers.

Do you sometimes feel inadequate explaining how prayer works, why it sometimes seems that our prayers aren't answered, and why we should pray if God already knows our needs? You'll appreciate the way these important fundamentals are explained in simple language kids can understand.

The classroom strategies and helpful hints presented in "Instant Helps and Handouts" will help make prayer a dynamic part of life in your classroom.

There's no greater privilege than teaching kids to talk to God. This is a valuable resource you'll turn to again and again as you lead kids in their journeys of faith.

Prayer From a Teacher's Heart

"Some people brought their little children to Jesus so he could touch them, but his followers told them to stop. When Jesus saw this, he was upset and said to them, 'Let the little children come to me. Don't stop them, because the kingdom of God belongs to people who are like these children. I tell you the truth, you must accept the kingdom of God as if you were a little child, or you will never enter it.' Then Jesus took the children in his arms, put his hands on them, and blessed them" (Mark 10:13-16).

During a lesson on love, a teacher assured her class, "Your dad and mom love you very much." During prayer time, four-year-old Randy prayed, "Dear God, I know Daddy loves me very much. But he doesn't come home anymore. Please bring my daddy home."

Teaching children about prayer is both a privilege and an incredible challenge. Look, for instance, at Randy's prayer above. Randy, a preschooler, already holds a graduate degree in faith and trust! Most young children do. But God won't manipulate Randy's father to suddenly appear at the front door of his house. Instead, God will allow Randy's father to make his own choice. If his father chooses not to come home, what can we say to Randy about prayer?

Prayer is as simple as talking to God and as complex as understanding that a sovereign God allows humans to exercise free will. The most learned theologian cannot pretend to understand the deep mysteries of prayer. So how can we hope to teach its complexities to children?

Take encouragement from the fact that as teachers, we are not the authors of our students' relationships with God. We are just the facilitators. God, through the Holy Spirit, will touch the heart of each child. The Holy Spirit will also come alongside us and teach us how to teach.

God has chosen to make prayer available to everyone. So we needn't feel inadequate to take children through their first steps in understanding prayer. There's a standing invitation for any citizen of this earth to approach the throne of grace—and to come boldly. Let's extend that invitation joyfully to the children God has put in our care. Hooray! Let's pray!

CHAPTER ONE

Hooray! Let's Pray! ● Hooray! Let's Pray! ● Hooray! Let's Pray!

BASIC PRINCIPLES OF PRAYER

We can begin by focusing briefly on four basic principles of prayer expressed in the acronym "ACTS": adoration, confession, thanksgiving, and supplication. We find these four elements of prayer throughout the Bible. Let's take a quick look at each of these key components of prayer and restate them in language kids can understand.

ADORATION

We could define adoration as deep love and admiration for God which inspires us to express praise and worship. Psalm 86:12-13 gives us a glimpse of David's adoration: "Lord, my God, I will praise you with all my heart, and I will honor your name forever. You have great love for me. You have saved me from death." For children, adoration means joyfully accepting God's love and, in turn, loving God!

CONFESSION

Sin throws a roadblock in our relationships with our holy God. Confession means acknowledging our sins and asking God's forgiveness for them. True confession involves determining that, with God's help, we'll seek to avoid committing the confessed sin again. Kids can easily understand confession as telling God we're sorry for the wrong things we've done. We can assure kids that when we tell God we're sorry, we can be confident of God's loving response. "But if we confess our sins, he will forgive our sins, because we can trust God to do what is right. He will cleanse us from all the wrongs we have done" (1 John 1:9).

THANKSGIVING

Thanksgiving is the discipline of recalling the good things God does for us and expressing our gratitude joyfully. As children mature, they can learn to be thankful in good times as well as difficult times by seeing and acknowledging God's power at work in situations beyond human control. Encourage children to practice "attitudes of gratitude" by watching for God's hand in their lives and giving thanks for blessings both large and small. "Thanks be to God for his gift that is too wonderful for words" (2 Corinthians 9:15).

SUPPLICATION

Supplication (definitely not a kid word!) means asking God to meet our needs and the needs of others. In exhorting the Philippian church, Paul says, "Do not worry about anything, but pray and ask God for everything you need, always giving thanks" (Philippians 4:6). God knows our needs before we ask, but he still wants us to ask. Why? Because when we ask, we acknowledge

CHAPTER ONE

Hooray! Let's Pray! ● Hooray! Let's Pray! ● Hooray! Let's Pray!

our dependence on God's provision. Asking places us in a humble relationship with our all-knowing, all-loving, all-powerful God.

We can teach children to express their love for God, to tell God they're sorry for the wrong things they've done, to say "thank you" for all the good things God does for them, and to ask God for the things they—and others—need. But what do we do when children feel that God isn't answering their prayers?

GOD HEARS

Let's turn back to God's Word. The Bible is crystal clear: our prayers are heard and answered in God's own time. Here's just a fraction of the happy evidence.

● "I prayed for this child, and the Lord answered my prayer and gave him to me" (1 Samuel 1:27).

● "When you first started praying, an answer was given, and I came to tell you, because God loves you very much" (Daniel 9:23a).

● "While Jonah was inside the fish, he prayed to the Lord his God and said,…'When my life had almost gone, I remembered the Lord. I prayed to you, and you heard my prayers in your Holy Temple'…Then the Lord spoke to the fish, and the fish threw up Jonah onto the dry land" (Jonah 2:1, 7, 10).

● "Elijah was a human being just like us. He prayed that it would not rain, and it did not rain on the land for three and a half years!" (James 5:17)

● "When a believing person prays, great things happen" (James 5:16b).

AND GOD ANSWERS

The problem with "unanswered" prayers is not that God is unwilling, unable, or uncaring. It is just that our anticipated answers and God's perfect answers may be quite different. The prophet Isaiah explains: "The Lord says, 'My thoughts are not like your thoughts. Your ways are not like my ways. Just as the heavens are higher than the earth, so are my ways higher than your ways and my thoughts higher than your thoughts' " (Isaiah 55:8-9).

God, with perfect wisdom, often answers our petitions in ways we could never imagine. And sometimes those answers are years in coming. We can assure children of this: God knows what's best for us and will work everything out in time. Children can understand that when their prayers are in line with what God wants for them, they may see an answer right away. But sometimes the answer is to wait, because God has a better idea.

Sometimes sin blocks an answer to prayer that seems to be perfectly in line with God's will. We can explain to children that, as much as

God loves us and wants the best for us, God doesn't force us to love him and do what's right. It's also important that kids learn to keep praying and not give up hope. Over time, God can soften the heart of even the most hardened person.

As children explore the Bible, they'll learn about the great power in prayer. But how will they learn that God's power is still at work in the world today? By hearing and sharing stories of faith. Be sure to tell kids what you're praying for, and how God is answering your prayers and the prayers of others in your family and congregation.

SETTING THE EXAMPLE

Faith ignites faith, and your witness can be the match that kindles a deep faith that will burn in your students for years to come. Much of what our students learn from us about prayer will be "caught" rather than taught. Our comfort level in speaking to God will inevitably affect our classes. If we teachers are models (and we are—like it or not!), how shall we pray? Let's examine a few simple, scriptural guidelines for prayer.

● **Speak to God as a friend.** We can speak to God as an intimate, revered friend. A children's worker who served as a missionary in Japan shared how moved she felt when she could finally understand these words with which her Japanese friends typically began their prayers: "tenno chi-chi naru kami-sama." The phrase roughly translates to "heavenly, most honored God who has become our daddy." The Japanese language is unique in its many levels of politeness. Most of the words of this phrase reflect the highest standard of polite, reverent language. The exception is, of course, "who has become our daddy."

When Jesus prayed in Gethsemane, he called God "Abba" (Mark 14:36), the Aramaic word for "Father" or "Daddy." Paul says in Romans 8:15, "For you did not receive a spirit that makes you a slave again to fear, but you received the Spirit of sonship. And by him we cry, 'Abba, Father'" (New International Version). Scripture clearly encourages us to develop an intimate relationship with our loving, omnipotent God. Our prayers need to reflect both that closeness and the reverence due to the awesome Creator of the universe.

● **Use simple, conversational language.** We need to keep our prayers direct and uncluttered. Jesus said, "And when you pray,

CHAPTER ONE

Hooray! Let's Pray! ● Hooray! Let's Pray! ● Hooray! Let's Pray!

don't be like those people who don't know God. They continue saying things that mean nothing, thinking that God will hear them
because of their many words" (Matthew 6:7). We've all heard elo-
quently spoken prayers that meant absolutely nothing. These prayers,
packed with flowery phrases and antiquated language, confuse and
discourage young pray-ers. Pray in language your children can
understand, and keep your prayers to the point. "Praying around the
world" is noble in many settings, but when you pack too much into
one prayer, kids will tend to fidget and lose their focus.

● **Be truthful and unmanipulative.** Our prayers need to be
honest. Don't thank God aloud for "the great kids in this class" if you
feel they've been acting like a bunch of hyenas! A more honest prayer
would be, "Lord, I'm really low on patience, and I need your help."

We need to scrupulously avoid manipulative prayers. It's easier
than you might imagine to slip into the habit of praying with a hidden agenda. The editor of a Christian magazine was both amused and
alarmed when her three-year-old began to use "prayer" to manipulate.
During a family TV night, little Abby disliked the program Mom had
chosen. "Please God," she prayed spontaneously. "Don't let Mommy
pick this program." A teacher's manipulative prayer might be, "Lord,
please help everyone be respectful and quiet today," or "Please help
Jamie and Jackie to get along." You might make those requests in private, but not in class. Children who feel scolded or "tattled on" by
prayer will not become willing pray-ers themselves.

● **Pray for your children in class.** Our prayers can show
our students that it's important to rely on God in difficult
moments. If a child becomes sick during class or shares a concern
about a loved one, it's appropriate to stop and pray right on the
spot. Kids learn from these prayers that God is always right there
with them, that it's important to "carry each other's burdens"
(Galatians 6:2, New International Version), and that even mature
adults depend on God's help.

We can pray for each child in our classes, and let them know
we're doing it. As class opens, it's always appropriate—especially
with younger children—to thank God for each child by name. If a
child has been absent because of illness or a vacation, it's a good
idea to thank God for his or her health and safe return. Thanking
God for visitors and praying that they'll enjoy the class and feel
right at home goes a long way toward putting new children at ease.

● **Pray for your children outside of class.** Of course,
there's no substitute for praying for students throughout the week.

Hooray! Let's Pray! ● Hooray! Let's Pray! ● Hooray! Let's Pray!

Kids love to receive cards in the mail that say, "I'll be praying for you to enjoy your piano recital," "I'm praying about a job for your dad," or "In my prayers today, I thanked God for you. I'm so glad you're part of my class!"

For most people, the daily discipline of prayer doesn't come easily. To keep your prayer life fresh and compelling, consider trying these creative prayer ideas as you pray for your children.

● Draw a large circle on a sheet of paper. Have children stamp their thumb prints around the circle and sign their names by their thumb prints. As you pray for each child, touch his or her thumb prints and thank God for what makes that child unique.

● Trace around a gingerbread-man cookie cutter on paper and cut out as many shapes as you have students. Write the name of a student on each shape. Tape the hands of the cookie shapes together to form a "garland of kids." Hang the garland where you'll see it each day. When you notice an area of growth or need in a child's life, note that on his or her cookie shape. Use your garland to keep track of how your students are growing in their relationships with God.

● Buy a package of Gummi bear candies and place them in a clear glass jar with a lid. As you take a Gummi bear, think of a child in your class. Pray for that child as you eat the Gummi bear. Then take another Gummi bear and pray for another child.

● Before you water your houseplants each week, read this promise from Isaiah: "Rain and snow fall from the sky and don't return without watering the ground. They cause the plants to sprout and grow, making seeds for the farmer and bread for the people. The same thing is true of the words I speak. They will not return to me empty. They make the things happen that I want to happen, and they succeed in doing what I send them to do" (Isaiah 55:10-11). As you water your plants, pray that God will cause the seeds of faith you're planting in children's lives to grow.

God bless you as you lead your students in experiencing the joy, the power, and the friendship with God that comes through prayer!

"Whoever accepts a child like this in my name accepts me. And whoever accepts me accepts the One who sent me" (Mark 9:37).

Childhood: The Season of Trust

"I tell you the truth, you must change and become like little children. Otherwise, you will never enter the kingdom of heaven. The greatest person in the kingdom of heaven is the one who makes himself humble like this child" (Matthew 18:3b-4).

After a lesson on forgiveness, four-year-old Scott prayed, "Dear God, please forgive me for doing wrong things, and please forgive Satan for all the wrong things he's done today, too."

Have you ever been astounded by the faith of a young child? Perhaps the more appropriate question is: Who *hasn't* been amazed, moved, and put to shame by the simple faith and surprising spiritual insights of young children? The basic yet profound prayers of children often move us to pray fervently, "Lord, teach us to pray."

When Jesus' disciples made the same request, Jesus was certainly up to the challenge! He knew intimately the hearts and minds of these twelve men who had traveled with him for nearly three years. If we are to do a good job of teaching our students to pray, we need to know their hearts and understand how their minds work. It's well worth our while to take a brief look not only at how kids learn but also at how kids learn *best*.

⌖ CHILD DEVELOPMENT

Jean Piaget and Abraham Maslow have laid a solid foundation of what educators can expect from children as they mature. Through their studies of human development, they've observed and interpreted a growth process that describes what kinds of intellectual tasks children will be able to do at different ages. Preschoolers dwell in the realm of the concrete. They need to see, smell, and touch in order to learn. As children approach the teen years and progress toward higher level thinking, they become more comfortable in the world of abstract ideas.

Are we wasting our time, then, trying to teach young children the abstract concept of prayer? Not at all! The path from concrete to critical thinking is not a lock step process. If you've ever taught multi-age groups, you've probably noticed that on any given day, the most profound insight may come from one of the younger learners. "Woo-hoo!" says a thoroughly impressed older child. "I never would have thought of that!"

MULTIPLE INTELLIGENCES

Adding to the complex picture of how kids learn is the issue of multiple intelligences. Many educators and human development experts believe that, from infancy, each of us is "wired" to learn in different ways. In order for individuals to understand new information, process it, and incorporate it into long-term memory, that information must come through the right channels. Traditional teaching methods that rely heavily on lecture and reading totally miss a huge percentage of kids. When we're teaching about prayer, we can't afford to miss anyone! We need to vary prayer activities so that we hit every intelligence and learning style.

The seven "roots of understanding" explained below are adapted from Howard Gardner's theory of multiple intelligences. As you read through them, take a moment to identify where each child in your class fits. You may want to pencil in names by the appropriate descriptions and then take note of what teaching methods will work best with each child.

● **Linguistic learners are word smart.** They enjoy listening, reading, writing, speaking, reasoning, and debating. They're usually good at memorization. These kids shine in traditional classrooms and often become teachers' pets!

To reach linguistic learners: Offer opportunities for reading and writing, and engage them in lively discussions. Let them assist you by asking questions to draw out less expressive students.

● **Logical learners are logic smart.** They like to observe, analyze, hypothesize, and solve problems. They're most comfortable in the cause-and-effect world of science, math, engineering, investigation, and law.

To reach logical learners: Clearly explain activities step-by-step, ask questions that require thought and analysis, and give opportunities for them to share their conclusions.

● **Visual learners are picture smart.** They enjoy all kinds of art and generally have vivid imaginations. Don't be surprised when you find them doodling—they may be using their gifts to interpret what they're learning.

CHAPTER TWO

Hooray! Let's Pray! ● Hooray! Let's Pray! ● Hooray! Let's Pray!

To reach visual learners: Splash colorful visuals all over your classroom. Keep art supplies readily accessible. Use interactive bulletin boards, maps, posters, and illustrated books. Let them work on open-ended art projects.

● **Musical learners are music smart.** They're full of rhythm and are more sensitive to sounds than other students. They may enjoy performing, even at a very early age.

To reach musical learners: Set the mood for activities with music. Teach with songs, raps, and cheers. Encourage them to lead musical activities, and to bring instruments and favorite recordings to class.

● **Bodily-kinesthetic learners are body smart.** They're agile, athletic, and always on the move. They enjoy touching and manipulating things and often end up in "hands-on" fields such as medicine, outdoor occupations, and mechanical or repair jobs.

To reach bodily-kinesthetic learners: Use active and interactive learning. Get them out of their chairs, even out of the classroom. Sandwich "sitting time" between more active-learning segments.

● **Introspective learners are self smart.** They're thoughtful, quiet, and aware of their strengths and weaknesses. While theirs may be the last hands to go up, their answers will often be the most insightful.

To reach introspective learners: Allow them quiet time to process new ideas and information. Speak to them one-on-one whenever possible. Let them choose less active roles. Respect their need to go at a more deliberate pace.

● **Interpersonal learners are people smart.** They're sociable beings, and are happiest "in the middle of things." They're good communicators and generally sensitive to other people's feelings.

To reach interpersonal learners: Provide opportunities to work in teams and small groups. Allow "chat" time before and after learning activities. Ask them to help new kids become acquainted with class members.

As you read through this information, did you recognize yourself? Which root of understanding best describes you? Do you tend to gravitate toward teaching activities that best complement your learning style? Here's a challenge: In order to reach all your kids, you'll need to step out of your comfort zone and employ teaching methods that work well for kids whose strengths are different from yours. This book offers dozens of creative prayer ideas that tap into each root of understanding. So vary your approach. Try ideas that seem a bit uncomfortable to you. Then you'll be teaching your kids the way God meant them to be taught.

LIFE TEACHES BEST

Sometimes life itself is the best teacher, because real life is never limited to reading and writing. Life experiences tap into every intelligence and learning style to teach children unforgettable lessons about prayer and faith. These heartwarming stories from parents and teachers illustrate how even young children sometimes step out of their prescribed zone of understanding to take the lead in faith issues.

Seven-year-old Josh had been a calm, curious observer during his grandfather's funeral and interment. Just before bedtime prayers, he asked, "What happens to Grandpa's body now?" His mother answered with a question: "What happens to the eggshell after a baby bird hatches?" Josh smiled and then prayed, "Dear God, thank you that Grandpa flew away to heaven to be with you!"

Nancy, a mom with three preschool boys, received a desperate phone call asking prayer for a premature baby named Ryan. Ryan was in intensive care with pneumonia and was not expected to live. Feeling devastated by her friend's news, Nancy turned to her children for prayer support. As they sat in a circle and held hands, Nancy's two-year-old volunteered to pray first. "God, help tiny Ryan to grow big, big, big like my daddy. Thank you for his eyes, nose, mouth, toes, feet, hands, ears, and everything."

Her three-year-old followed with, "Dear Jesus, would you please make Ryan all better?" Finally, the five-year-old added, "Heavenly Father, thank you for your perfect timing. If you hadn't had Ryan be born sooner than he was supposed to, he would have drowned for sure, having pneumonia and floating in the water inside his mom. Please take the water out of him so he can breathe better."

As Nancy watched her three young sons run off to play, she marveled at both the simplicity and the theological depth of their prayers. The two-year-old began with praise and focused on God's power. The three-year-old acknowledged Jesus' healing power and simply asked that Ryan would get well. The five-year-old affirmed his trust in God's wisdom. What adults labeled "premature," he saw as "God's perfect timing." You can imagine Nancy's joy a few days later when

CHAPTER TWO

Hooray! Let's Pray! ● Hooray! Let's Pray! ● Hooray! Let's Pray!

she announced to her trio of mini-prayer-warriors, "Ryan is well!"

One family has passed down through generations a precious story of a child's faith. Their pioneer ancestors eked out a meager existence farming a poor homestead in South Dakota at the turn of the century. Food was scarce, so when the sweet corn crop was harvested, they feasted royally. Later that evening, three-year-old Lois became gravely ill. The family summoned the doctor. He said that her colic from eating too much fresh corn could prove fatal. The young pioneer couple kept watch and prayed at their daughter's bedside far into the night. In the wee hours of the morning, the toddler sat up in bed as a huge smile broke across her face. "Look!" she cried. "Can you see the angels? Listen to them sing!" Then she lay back on the rough-hewn bed and died with a beautiful smile of anticipation on her face.

EARLY LEARNING CAN LEAD TO SOLID, EARLY FAITH

Precocious faith can also lead to unexpected faith crises. A pastor's wife tells the story of how her first-grade daughter, Christy, struggled with prayer. "How can I know God is even there?" she challenged. "And if God is there, how do I know he's listening to me? I don't feel like praying any more!"

Determined not to show her shock, the mother asked calmly, "How about if I pray and you just listen?" Christy agreed. When the mother recounted Christy's doubts to her husband, they both marveled at their daughter's way-too-early faith crisis. "How can this be happening to our six-year-old?" they wondered. "She isn't supposed to think that way until she's a teenager!"

For several weeks the parents prayed as their daughter listened dubiously. Then one day Christy ran from the school bus and burst into the house shouting, "I can pray now! I know God is real because he sat right beside me on the bus!"

"What happened?" asked the astounded mother.

The child replied, "I was humming 'I love you Lord and I lift my voice' when suddenly I got all warm and it was like God was giving me a big hug! I just knew God was there, Mommy, and he was real!"

Children are full of surprises. No wonder Jesus said, "I praise you, Father, Lord of heaven and earth, because you have hidden these things from the people who are wise and smart. But you have shown them to those who are like little children" (Luke 10:21b).

Hooray! Let's Pray! ● Hooray! Let's Pray! ● Hooray! Let's Pray!

⊚ BE A TEACHER-LEARNER

A child's instinctive faith is a precious gift. Jesus affirmed this when he said, "Let the little children come to me. Don't stop them, because the kingdom of heaven belongs to people who are like these children" (Matthew 19:14). In fact, Jesus urged his followers to seek a childlike faith: "I tell you the truth, you must change and become like little children. Otherwise, you will never enter the kingdom of heaven" (Matthew 18:3).

Wise teachers, then, need to be teacher-learners. While we feed students the "milk" of God's Word, we can learn from them what it means to trust God wholeheartedly, to pray in simple faith, and to purge our minds of the adult plagues of cynicism, bitterness, and the egocentric desire to rule our own fate.

Certainly the traditionally taught stages of learning and development give parents and teachers an excellent frame of reference for what to expect from children as their thinking skills and understanding of the world develop. But when it comes to matters of prayer and faith, don't be surprised if your students surprise you! It's so important to respect the faith of our young learners. What a delight it is when the Holy Spirit turns the tables on us, making us the learners and the children our teachers!

"The leading priests and the teachers of the law saw that Jesus was doing wonderful things and that the children were praising him in the Temple, saying, 'Praise to the Son of David.' All these things made the priests and the teachers of the law very angry. They asked Jesus, 'Do you hear the things these children are saying?' Jesus answered, 'Yes. Haven't you read in the Scriptures, "You have taught children and babies to sing praises"?'" (Matthew 21:15-16).

Ready, Set, Pray!

"One time Jesus was praying in a certain place. When he finished, one of his followers said to him, 'Lord, teach us to pray'" (Luke 11:1a).

A teacher asked her Sunday school class, "Who would like to pray for this special Passover meal?" Five-year-old Allison raised her hand enthusiastically. "I will!" she said. "Thank you, dear Lord, for this special pacifier supper we are about to eat."

Children who have been raised in praying homes seem to pray almost instinctively, but those who encounter prayer for the first time in a church setting may be confused and skeptical about the idea of talking to God. Kids of all ages and backgrounds need to mature in their understanding of prayer by learning foundational truths about prayer from the Bible. Use these active-learning ideas to help kids understand what happens when we pray, and why it's important to stay in communication with our loving God.

A ROYAL INVITATION

Truth: God invites us to speak to him any time, anywhere.

Make one photocopy of the "Invitations" handout (p. 25) for each child, and cut out the invitations. Give each child a "presidential" invitation. If you have nonreaders, ask a volunteer to read the invitation aloud. Then ask:
● **Would you be surprised to receive this invitation? Why or why not?**
● **What would you wear for a visit to the White House?**
● **What kinds of things would you say to the president?**
Say: **I have another invitation for each of you.** Hand out the "heavenly" invitations. Ask:
● **What does this invitation mean to you?**
● **Have you ever visited God's throne room before? Tell about your visit.**
● **What do you wear when you speak to God?**
Say: **Listen to how a king responded to God's heavenly invitation.** Have a volunteer read 2 Kings 19:14-16 aloud. Ask:

CHAPTER THREE

Hooray! Let's Pray! ● Hooray! Let's Pray! ● Hooray! Let's Pray!

● **How did King Hezekiah talk to God?**
● **Do we need to use fancy words when we pray? Explain.**
Say: **Even though God is far more powerful than any king or president, God invites us to speak to him any time, any place. We don't need to put on beautiful clothes, say fancy words, or even brush our teeth! God loves us and wants us to pray. God even promises to help us if we don't know how to pray!**

Have a volunteer read Romans 8:26 aloud. Ask another child to close with a simple prayer thanking God for hearing our prayers and for helping us when we don't know how to pray. Encourage kids to keep their heavenly invitations as prayer reminders.

⊚ COMING YOUR WAY

Truth: Prayer helps us tune in to God's plans for our lives.

Have kids form pairs. Distribute blindfolds, and have one partner in each pair blindfold the other. Have seeing partners guide their blindfolded partners to stand against a wall of the classroom. Then ask the seeing partners to stand five or six feet away.

Put a pile of tossable objects on the floor near the seeing partners. Include items such as soft foam balls, small pillows, rolled-up newspapers, and sock rolls.

Say: **We're going to play a game called Coming Your Way. Here's how it works. Partners who can see will choose any of the items in this pile on the floor to toss very gently to their blindfolded partners. They won't give any clues about what they're tossing. Just before they toss, they'll say, "Coming your way!" and their partner's name. Toss carefully—you want your partner to catch as many times as possible. Ready? Go!**

After each toss, have the seeing partners retrieve the items and place them in the pile for other students to toss. After four or five tosses, have partners change roles. After four or five more tosses, call time. Set the items and blindfolds aside, and ask:
● **Who was able to catch one item? two? three? four?**
● **What was it like trying to catch something that you couldn't see?**
● **What would've made it easier?**
● **How was this game like what happens in real life when problems come our way?**

Say: **We don't know what life will bring us, but God does!** Have a volunteer read Jeremiah 29:11-13 aloud.

CHAPTER THREE

Hooray! Let's Pray! ● Hooray! Let's Pray! ● Hooray! Let's Pray!

● **How is God like the tosser in our game?**
● **What does God promise to do for us?**
● **What does it mean to seek God with all your heart?**

Say: **God knows what's coming our way. When we pray, it's important to tune in to God and to listen as well as speak. God has good plans for each of us, and praying helps us discover those plans.**

Pray: **Lord, thank you for your loving plans for our lives. Help us to seek you with all our hearts. In Jesus' name, amen.**

Adapted from *Sunday School Specials 2*. Copyright © Lois Keffer. Published by Group Publishing, Inc., P.O. Box 481, Loveland, CO 80539. Used by permission.

AND THE ANSWER IS...

Truth: God always answers our prayers the very best way.

Cut apart the answer slips (p. 26). Place each slip in a balloon; then blow up the balloons and tie them. You'll need one balloon for each child. (If you'd rather not use balloons, simply place the slips in a basket.)

Set out a tray of yummy-looking treats. Say: **I know you'd all like to enjoy these treats, and I'm going to give you a chance to do that. Form a line in front of me. When I come to you, ask, "May I please have a treat?" Then we'll see what happens.**

When the first child asks, "May I please have a treat?" say: **Choose a balloon, and pop it to find your answer.** Let each child in turn pop a balloon.

Let kids who get positive responses enjoy treats. Tell the other kids not to give up hope. Then gather everyone in a circle on the floor. Ask:

● **Do you think I've been fair with everyone? Why or why not?**

Say: **There are times when we want something so badly that it's all we can think about. That happened to Abraham and Sarah, whose story we find in the book of Genesis in the Bible. God had promised Abraham he would be the father of many nations. But Abraham and his wife never had any children. They prayed and prayed for a son, year after year. They didn't understand why God would make such a promise and then not give them any children. One day when Abraham and Sarah were very old, three visitors came to Abraham's tent and made another promise. Let's find out what happened.**

Have a volunteer read Genesis 18:9-14. Ask:
● **Why do you think Sarah laughed?**
Say: **Let's read what happened a few months later.** Have a volunteer read aloud Genesis 21:1-7. Then ask:
● **Why did Sarah laugh this time?**
Say: **Abraham and Sarah waited a long time for a son, and some of you have waited a long time for a treat. If you haven't had a treat yet, please help yourself.** Ask:
● **How did God answer Sarah and Abraham's prayers?**
● **How are the answers you got from the balloons like the answers God gives us when we pray? How are they different?**
● **Why doesn't God always answer "yes"?**
Say: **When you popped the balloon and read the slip of paper, chance determined whether you'd have to wait or whether you'd get a treat immediately. But when we pray, we can be confident God hears and answers us according to what's best for us.**

When it seems God isn't answering our prayers, or when we get an answer we don't want, we sometimes get discouraged, or think that God isn't fair. But God loves us more than we can imagine, and he knows what's best. Whether God answers "yes," "no," or "wait," we can always trust God to do what's best for us.

Ask a volunteer to pray and thank God for always giving the best answers to our prayers.

◎DO YOUR PART!
Truth: God wants us to pray for each other.

Set a fairly large table at one end of a room, and gather kids around it. Say: **I need a volunteer to carry this table to the other end of the room. The person who does it will win a special surprise.** After you've chosen a volunteer, say: **I'm sorry to report that you have nine broken fingers. You'll only be able to carry this table with one finger. And, by the way—you may not drag the table. You must lift it and carry it all the way there.**

Allow several seconds to pass. When the volunteer gives up, ask for another volunteer. Put the same restrictions on him or her. Then announce: **Everyone in this room has nine broken fingers, including me! It looks like we're going to have a problem getting this table to the other end of the room. Let's see if the**

CHAPTER THREE

Hooray! Let's Pray! ● Hooray! Let's Pray! ● Hooray! Let's Pray!

Bible has any advice for us.

Have volunteers look up and read aloud 1 Samuel 12:23; Romans 15:30; and Galatians 6:2. Then ask:

● **What do all these verses have in common?**

● **How can what we learned in these verses help us get the table to the other end of the room?**

Kids will probably realize that if they all use one finger, they can carry the table easily. After you've helped the class move the table, ask:

● **When do people need the support of their friends?**

● **What are some ways we can support each other?**

Say: **We're not always able to help people in need by giving them money, making dinner for them, or helping repair their cars. But there is one thing we can always do.** Ask:

● **How can we always help each other?**

Say: **Praying is the most important way to help. Sometimes there are other helping things we can do, but we can always start with prayer.** Have children gather around the table and lift it with their fingers again. As they are holding it, pray: **Dear Lord, thank you for the good things you teach us in the Bible. Help us remember to help each other with our prayers. In Jesus' name, amen.**

Say: **Now for the good surprise I mentioned earlier. All of our fingers have healed! Let's stand in a circle; then each of you turn to your right, and give a shoulder rub to the person in front of you.**

PAL PRAYERS

Truth: Listening is an important part of prayer.

Have kids form two groups of equal size. If you have an uneven number of kids, join one of the groups yourself. Ask one group to step outside the room and wait quietly for you to come and give them instructions.

Huddle with the remaining group, and say: **When the other group comes back into the room, I'll say "go." Then each of you must try to get someone from the other group to sing "Happy Birthday to You." You'll have thirty seconds. It's very important that you get someone to do this in just thirty seconds, so don't waste any time!**

Then go to the group that's waiting outside the room, and say: **When you go back in the room, each of you must try to get someone from the other group to do ten jumping jacks. You'll have thirty seconds from the time I say "go." It's very important that you get someone to do this in just thirty seconds, so don't waste any time! Please follow me back into the room and wait for my signal.**

Lead the group back into the room, and shout: **Go!** Call time after thirty seconds, and gather everyone in a circle. Ask:

● **Did anyone accomplish the task I gave you? Why not?**

Say: **OK, let's try a different approach. When I say "go," find a partner from your own group, and see if you can accomplish your tasks. This time you'll have two minutes. Go!**

Call time after two minutes or when all the kids have accomplished their tasks. Then gather kids in a circle, and ask:

● **How many of you accomplished your tasks this time?**

● **Why were you successful this time but not the first time?**

● **How was the first, unsuccessful experience like what happens sometimes when we pray?**

Say: **Listen to what the Bible says about prayer.** Read aloud Psalm 46:10 (NIV).

Ask:

● **Why is it hard to listen when we pray?**

Say: **It's so easy to pray "gimme prayers." We say, "Lord, gimme this," and "Lord, gimme that." But maybe God has something to tell us. If we don't take time to listen, we may miss out on a really important message. I have a fun handout that will help you remember how to pray.**

Distribute tape or glue sticks, and photocopies of the "PAL Prayer Pyramid" handout (p. 27). Have kids cut out, fold, and tape or glue the pyramid. Then ask:

● **Why is it important to praise God when we pray?**

● **Why is it important to ask God to take care of our needs and the needs of other people?**

● **Why is it important to listen when we pray?**

Point out that the first letters of "praise," "ask," and "listen" form the acronym "PAL." Encourage kids to use their PAL Prayer Pyramids to help them when they pray.

THE BIG SQUEEZE
Truth: We need to set aside time to pray.

You'll need permanent markers, ten to fifteen large balloons, and a medium-sized garbage bag that will be too small to hold the balloons when they're all inflated.

Say: **First I'll need two or three windy volunteers to blow up these balloons.** Choose volunteers, and give each of them a few balloons. If you think some children will have difficulty blowing up balloons, inflate the balloons before class begins.

Then say: **And I'll need one or two scribes to write on the balloons.** Give each scribe a permanent marker.

Say: **Great! Now we're ready to begin. Let's name all the different things you do in a typical twenty-four-hour day. We'll write each activity on a balloon.**

Encourage kids to name activities such as getting dressed, eating, going to school, and talking on the phone. If no one mentions praying, be sure to bring it up yourself.

When most of the balloons are inflated, say: **Wow! It looks like we're busy people.** Hold up the garbage bag. **Let's pretend this is a day and see if we can get all these activities inside it.**

Begin putting balloons in the bag. Make sure the balloon labeled "pray" is the last one to go in. Look concerned and say: **If I try to stuff this balloon in the bag, I won't be able to close it. Hmm. Maybe we should leave this balloon out.** Ask:
● **What do you think we should do?**
● **How is this like what happens in real life?**
● **When Jesus lived on earth, do you think he was as busy as we are? Explain.**

Say: **Crowds of people followed Jesus everywhere he went. They wanted to hear Jesus teach, and they wanted him to heal sick friends and family members. Jesus was a busy, busy man. But listen to what he did.**

Read Luke 6:12 aloud. Ask:
● **How could Jesus find time to pray?**
● **How can we find time to pray?**
● **Why is it important to make time to pray every day?**

Say: **Jesus made time to pray because he knew how important it was to talk to his heavenly Father. We need to make time to pray, too, or else prayer will get squeezed right out of our lives. Turn to a partner and talk about a time of day you could set aside for prayer.**

Close with a prayer similar to this one: **Lord, sometimes our days are so busy that prayer gets squeezed out. Please help us to set aside a special time each day for prayer. In Jesus' name, amen.**

23

⊙ NO WORRIES

Truth: God wants us to pray instead of worrying.

You'll need a stack of newspapers and a large garbage bag. Gather kids in a circle with the stack of newspapers in the middle.

Hold the empty garbage bag, and say: **Today we're going to talk about worries. One thing I worry about is**_____. As you finish the sentence, crumple a newspaper and stuff it in the garbage bag. Then pass the bag to the person on your right. Have that person state a worry, crumple a sheet of newspaper, and stuff it in the bag. Reassure kids that it's fine if they mention similar worries. Keep passing the bag until it's full or until kids run out of ideas.

Tie the top of the bag, and say: **Hmm. This doesn't seem very heavy right now. Let's see if that changes.**

Have kids stand shoulder to shoulder in a tight circle and hold their arms straight out in front of them, palms up. Place the bag on kids' hands. Make sure kids don't lean or rest their arms on each other. If you have more than a dozen kids, simply have kids hold their arms out and imagine that all their worries are resting on their hands.

Say: **While you're holding that position, I'd like to read to you what Jesus says about worry.** Read Matthew 6:25-34 aloud, slowly and deliberately. Then ask:

● **What does Jesus want us to do with our worries?**

Say: **Drop your arms and shake them out. Feel the relief as you let go of your worries. There's another important Bible passage that tells us what to do about our worries.** Read aloud Philippians 4:6-7. Ask:

● **What does this passage tell us to do instead of worrying?**
● **What does it say will happen when we pray?**

Say: **Let's get rid of all those worries we just talked about. We'll go around the circle and take turns finishing this prayer. "Lord, please take away my worries about**_____.**"** Begin the prayer. When each child has finished the sentence, pray: **Lord, each time we worry, help us remember that we can choose to pray instead. Please fill our hearts with the peace you promised. In Jesus' name, amen.**

Close by emptying the bag and letting children stomp on the newspaper "worries."

HANDOUT

Hooray! Let's Pray! ● Hooray! Let's Pray! ● Hooray! Let's Pray!

Invitations

The president of the United States cordially invites you to visit the White House in Washington, D.C., on Great Kids' Day. The president wants to hear your concerns and wants to understand what's important to you. He has taken a personal interest in your future and wants to offer you his help and advice. R.S.V.P.

You are cordially invited to an audience with God almighty, creator of the universe. You may speak with His Majesty at your convenience— any time day or night. The way to God has been opened to you by the prince of peace, Jesus Christ. Don't worry about what you'll say to the King of Heaven. God has sent his Holy Spirit to be your helper and comforter. The Spirit will guide your conversation with God, and speak for you when you don't know what to say. His Majesty offers this invitation because he loves you and wants to offer you help and guidance. R.S.V.P.

HANDOUT

Hooray! Let's Pray! ● Hooray! Let's Pray! ● Hooray! Let's Pray!

Answer Slips

Of course! Help yourself!

Of course! Help yourself!

Of course! Help yourself!

Of course! Help yourself!

Of course! Help yourself!

Not right now—maybe later.

Not right now—maybe later.

Not right now—maybe later.

Not right now—maybe later.

Not right now—maybe later.

HANDOUT

Hooray! Let's Pray! ● Hooray! Let's Pray! ● Hooray! Let's Pray!

PAL Prayer Pyramid

Cut out the pattern on the solid line; then crease the dotted lines.
Fold the pattern into a pyramid shape and secure it with glue or tape.

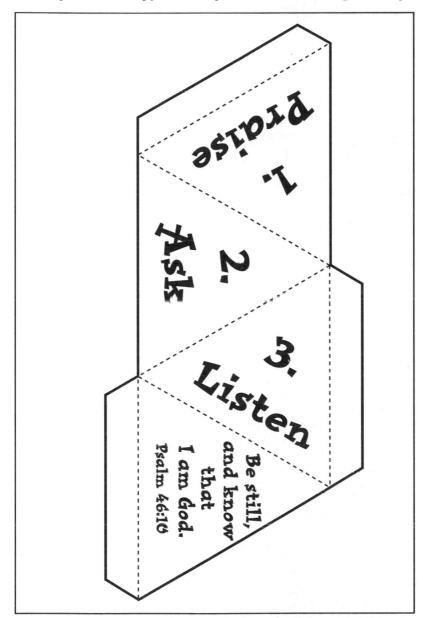

Praying With Preschoolers

"Be careful. Don't think these little children are worth nothing. I tell you that they have angels in heaven who are always with my Father in heaven" (Matthew 18:10).

Before prayer time, a preschool teacher reminded her class that "Jesus can take away our pain." Five-year-old Emily wanted to pray first. "Dear God," she prayed solemnly, "I thank you that Mom isn't having any more pain since she had her nose job."

Jesus has a special place in his heart for little children. When the disciples tried to shoo away parents who brought their children to be blessed, Jesus said, "Let the little children come to me. Don't stop them, because the kingdom of heaven belongs to people who are like these children" (Matthew 19:14). Jesus interrupted his conversation with adults (which the disciples mistakenly took to be more important), took the children in his arms, and blessed them.

Young children have innocent desires to draw near to God. They seem to be able to talk to God about anything, as the anecdote above illustrates! Once preschoolers have a basic understanding that there is a God who listens to their prayers, they're eager to pray. It's our responsibility to carefully nourish this desire. Jesus cautioned his followers not to hinder children or cause them to sin. Ours is the joyful task of encouraging little ones to climb into Jesus' lap and learn to pray.

Does that imply we should expect little ones to sit totally still, hands folded, and eyes closed during prayer time? Hardly. Closing our eyes does have the benefit of reducing visual distractions. And it's a discipline preschoolers can begin to build gradually. But our omniscient, omnipresent God who makes children and understands them certainly would not require that little ones assume a formal posture in order for their prayers to be heard. In fact, the only time Scripture refers to folding hands is in Proverbs 6:10-11 which states: "You sleep a little; you take a nap. You fold your hands and lie down to rest. So you will be as poor as if you had been robbed."

Throughout Scripture we find references to a variety of postures of prayer. Psalm 47:1 tells us to clap our hands. Psalm 134:2 mentions raising up our hands in the Temple. First Timothy 2:8 again mentions lifting our hands in prayer. Second Samuel 6:14a states that "David danced with all his might before the Lord." The Living Bible gives this paraphrase of David's explanation in verse 21: "I am willing to act like a fool in order to show my joy in the Lord." In light of these biblical examples, it doesn't seem out of line to suggest that preschoolers

CHAPTER FOUR

Hooray! Let's Pray! ● Hooray! Let's Pray! ● Hooray! Let's Pray!

should have many opportunities to pray to God in ways that come naturally to them!

A mother with many years of experience teaching preschoolers confessed that when her own daughter was very young, she was expected to sit still, close her eyes, and fold her hands for prayer. The mother also confessed to peeking to see if her daughter was complying. Of course, she wasn't. And she continued not to do so right through her college years. Yet, this wiggly child developed a deep, personal relationship with God as attested to by her volumes of prayer journals.

As preschoolers begin to form their concepts of God, we want them to think of God as a friend or parent they can converse with spontaneously and naturally. But how can little ones, being concrete thinkers, relate to a someone they can't see? Fortunately God gave us a visual aid—Jesus!

Teaching small children to pray requires meeting them at their level of interest and understanding. We reach young minds through the avenues of sight, sound, smell, and touch. Therefore, children learn best in an environment full of appealing sensory stimuli such as colorful Bible story pictures, dolls, and other huggable and touchable toys.

The following pages offer a great variety of active, sensory prayer experiences for preschoolers. Have a wonderful time leading your little ones in their first steps toward God!

◎ TOY THANKS

Truth: We give thanks for God's good gifts.

Let children each find a favorite classroom toy to carry to your prayer area. Say: **God likes to hear us say "thank you" for the things that make us happy.** Let children take turns holding up their toys and saying "Thank you, God." After everyone has prayed, lead children in marching around the room with their toys. Teach this rhyme as you march.

Thank you, God,
For these toys.
We are happy
Girls and boys!

Hooray! Let's Pray! ● Hooray! Let's Pray! ● Hooray! Let's Pray!

◎ PRAYER FINGERS

Truth: We thank God for loving us, helping us grow, and taking us to heaven.

You'll need yellow, brown, red, and green nontoxic markers. You'll also need clear nail polish. Have children sit in a circle around you and hold out one hand. As you color children's thumbnails yellow, say: **God loves us and wants us to live in heaven with him. Heaven is a happy place, so we use yellow to thank God for heaven. Let's pray, "Thank you, God, for heaven."** Have children repeat the simple prayer.

Color the nails of the children's index fingers brown, and say: **Sometimes we do wrong things. Wrong things make us dirty inside, and they make God sad. Brown is the color of dirt. Let's pray, "We're sorry, God."** Have children repeat.

As you color red hearts on the nails of their middle fingers, say: **Jesus loves us and wants to take away the bad things we do. Red hearts show how much Jesus loves us. Let's pray, "We love you, Jesus."** Have children repeat.

As you paint the nails of their ring fingers with clear nail polish, say: **Jesus' love makes us all clean inside. This polish is shiny and clean. Let's pray, "Thank you for making us clean."** Have children repeat.

As you color the nails of their pinkie fingers green, say: **Jesus will help us grow up strong, like tall green trees. Let's pray, "Jesus, help us grow" as we wiggle all our prayer fingers.** Have children repeat.

◎ SEE AND TOUCH PRAYER

Truth: Everything we see reminds us to give thanks.

Cut scraps of different-colored paper into pieces no smaller than two inches square. Collect scraps of material of different textures. Place the paper and the material scraps in a bag. Let each child pick an item from the bag and say a prayer of thanks to God for something that is the same color, or something that feels like what he or she is holding. For instance, he or she might thank God for the blue sky, a fuzzy bunny, a shiny red apple, or a soft doll.

CHAPTER FOUR

Hooray! Let's Pray! ● Hooray! Let's Pray! ● Hooray! Let's Pray!

SNACK TIME PRAYER

Truth: God is the one who gives us good food.

Teach children this simple rhyming prayer. Say it with the children each time you serve snacks.

Thank you for the food so good.
Help us eat the things we should.
A-men!

HIDE-AND-SEEK PRAYER

Truth: God cares for us.

Before class, wrap several small objects that show how God cares for us. For instance, you might wrap a package of crackers, a small plastic house, small stuffed "pets," a pair of socks, a favorite toy, and dolls that can portray family members. Wrap one object for each child, and hide the wrapped packages around the room.

Say: **God gives us good gifts every day. You can find some of those gifts in packages I've hidden. When you find a package, bring it back to our circle. Then we'll open our gifts and thank God together.**

After children have opened the packages, pray: **Dear God, thank you for taking care of us every day. Thank you for food and places to live and our families. We love you. Amen.**

SPOTLIGHT PRAYERS

Truth: There are special quiet times to thank God.

You'll need a flashlight, a candle with a hurricane shade, matches, a recording of soft worship music, and a cassette or CD player. Dim the lights and play the worship music. Gather the children in a circle on the floor, place the candle in the center of the circle, and light the candle.

Say: **This is a special time to be quiet. No one may touch our candle—it's just to look at. I will shine my flashlight on one person at a time. When my light shines on you, you can**

CHAPTER FOUR

Hooray! Let's Pray! ● Hooray! Let's Pray! ● Hooray! Let's Pray!

tell God one thing you're thankful for. You might say, "Thank you, God, for my dad," or "Thank you, God, for my house."

After each child has had a turn in the spotlight, blow out the candle and have all the children say "Amen!"

JUMPING PRAYER

Truth: There are special lively times to thank God.

Form two groups, and have them crouch down. Say: **We're going to learn a jumping game that will help us tell God that we love him. God likes us to praise him with our whole bodies.**

Teach Group 1 to say, "Thank you, thank you, God."

Teach Group 2 to say, "We love you, love you, God."

Say: **When I point to your group, jump up and say your words; then crouch back down as fast as you can.**

Alternate pointing to the two groups. With older preschoolers, vary the prayer by giving them extra cues such as "soft," "loud," "fast," and "slow." End by saying: **Everyone jump up and shout, "We love you, God!"**

PRAYER BALL*

Truth: We can thank God for others.

Gather children on the floor in a circle. Say: **We're going to talk to God. We talk to God when we pray, and God hears us. God is right here with us even though we can't see him. Right now I'm going to say a prayer and thank God for each one of you.** Roll the ball to a child and say: **Thank you, God for** (child's name). **I am glad** (name) **could be here.**

Have that child roll the ball to the next child in the circle. Thank God for that child, and have him or her roll it to another child. Continue until you've thanked God for everyone. When you've thanked God for all the children, have everyone join you in shouting: **Amen!**

CHAPTER FOUR

Hooray! Let's Pray! ● Hooray! Let's Pray! ● Hooray! Let's Pray!

BIBLE PRAYER

Truth: We can thank God for the Bible.

Have the children place their hands together and then open them like a book while you say this prayer:

The Bible is God's special book,
His words are written there.
And when I turn the page to look,
I learn of love and prayer.
Thank you, God, for the Bible!

PRAYER PARTNERS

Truth: God gives us friends we can pray with.

You'll need cards that have pictures of animals on them. Be sure to have two cards for each kind of animal. Stack the cards face down. Have each child draw a card. Say: **Move around our room, making the sound of the animal you picked. If your animal hops or crawls, you can move like that, too. Look for the person who is making the same animal sound you are making. That person will be your partner. Give your partner a hug, then come sit down together for prayer time.**
Lead children in praying: **Thank you, God, for my partner.**

DRESS-UP PRAYERS

Truth: We can pray for others.

You'll need a collection of dress-up clothes. Include play tools and hats representing various occupations. Let children dress up with the items of their choice and tell about the people who would wear the clothes they've chosen.
Say: **Let's pray for these people. Each of you can pray for a person who would wear or use what you picked today. God likes when we pray for other people.**

Hooray! Let's Pray! ● Hooray! Let's Pray! ● Hooray! Let's Pray!

AROUND-THE-WORLD PRAYERS

Truth: We can pray for people in other lands.

You'll need a globe or large map of the world, a blindfold, and stickers. Say: **This is a globe. It represents the world that God made. All of the different countries in which people live are shown on the globe. Here's our country.** Point to your country on the globe.

Give stickers to the children one at a time, blindfold the children, spin them around, and let them place their stickers on the map. As you spin the children, say this rhyme:

God is here; God is there;
God made our world. God's everywhere!

After a child has placed a sticker, help him or her say this prayer: **God bless the people in** (name of area).

After children pray, you may want to give them a few pennies, then collect their "offering" for missions.

FINGER-RHYME PRAYERS

Truth: We can pray for others.

This happy little finger rhyme will teach children to pray for others.

See my hands. They help me so. (Hold up both hands.)
Wiggly fingers—watch them go! (Wiggle fingers.)

When I talk to God, I pray. (Fold hands.)
Each one tells me what to say. (Touch fingertips together.)

Thumbs are oh-so-close to me. (Touch thumbs to chest.)
I'll pray for my family.

Pointer tells me what to do. (Shake index finger.)
I'll pray for my teacher, too.

Middle stands so tall, not bent. (Hold one hand upright. Hold the other hand flat on top of it.)
I'll pray for our president.

Rings for finger number four. *(Touch tips of fourth fingers.)*
Please bless the sick and weak and poor.

Little finger—small to see. *(Wiggle pinkies.)*
Now, I think I'll pray for me!

Adapted from *Fun to Learn Bible Lessons for Preschoolers, Volume 2.* Copyright © Nancy
Paulson. Published in *Hooray! Let's Pray!* by Group Publishing, Inc., P.O. Box 481, Loveland,
CO 80539. Used by permission.

ARTISTIC ADORATION
Truth: Prayer is talking to Jesus.

Ask children to tell you what they know about God; then invite them to draw pictures of Jesus.

Say: **We can take turns holding our pictures of Jesus for everyone to see. When you're showing your Jesus picture, you can talk to Jesus about anything that's important to you. You can tell Jesus you love him, you can thank Jesus for something, or you can tell Jesus about something that makes you sorry or happy.**

After all the children have displayed their pictures and prayed, invite them to hang their Jesus pictures at home. Explain that they can talk to Jesus any time because he's with them everywhere they go.

PICTURE PRAYERS
Truth: We can give thanks to God.

Before class, gather magazines and catalogs, and cut out pictures of items that are familiar to children. Mount the pictures on index cards or heavy paper and place them in a basket. At prayer time, pass the basket and invite the children to take pictures of their choice. Say: **You can say a thank-you prayer to God by telling him what you like about the thing you're holding.** When each child has had a turn, teach this simple prayer song to the tune of "Mary Had a Little Lamb."

Hooray! Let's Pray! ● Hooray! Let's Pray! ● Hooray! Let's Pray!

Thank you for this happy thing.
It makes me laugh; it makes me sing.
Thank you for this happy thing.
I love you, Lord!

PHONE THE FATHER

Truth: Prayer is talking to a God who always listens.

You'll need a banana for each child. Hand out the bananas, and ask:
● **Do you sometimes talk on the phone? Who do you talk to?**
Say: **Talking to God when we pray is like talking on the phone. God always has time to talk to you. You can pretend your banana is a phone and use it to talk to God right now. God can hear you, even when lots of other people are praying, too.**
After prayer time, have a banana-phone snack.

SUPPER WITH THE SAVIOR

Truth: We pray to God at mealtime.

You'll need tuna salad, crackers, and napkins. Spread a blanket on the floor for a pretend picnic. Include in your circle a person dressed like Jesus or a Jesus doll.
Tell the story from John 21:12-14 of how Jesus prepared breakfast for his disciples. Give each child tuna salad and crackers on a napkin. Invite children to tell Jesus about times they have had special meals on beaches or in campgrounds. Close by having the children tell Jesus what they like about him.

Hooray! Let's Pray! ● Hooray! Let's Pray! ● Hooray! Let's Pray!

JESUS IS MY FRIEND

Truth: Prayer shows our friendship with Jesus.

Use this rhyme to open your prayer time. Sing it to the tune of "The Farmer in the Dell."

Jesus is my friend.
Jesus is my friend.
When I come to him in prayer,
I know he's always there.

JESUS LOVES ME

Truth: Prayer shows our love for Jesus.

Add this second verse to "Jesus Loves Me." Encourage children to sing the song as a prayer.

I love Jesus; does he know?
Have I ever told him so?
I will come to him to pray
And show I love him every day.
Yes, I love Jesus.
Yes, I love Jesus.
Yes, I love Jesus.
I love him every day.

QUIET-TIME PRAYER

Truth: We thank God for watching over us.

Use this action prayer to help children make a transition from play time to rest time.

Thank you for this special day *(fold hands)*,
With time to laugh and eat and play. *(Clap four times in rhythm.)*

39

I stretch up high and turn around. *(Stretch arms over head and turn around.)*
Now I'm drifting slowly down *(turn around and slowly lie down),*
As I rest so quietly. *(Fold hands on chest.)*
Please, dear Lord, watch over me.

SHARING PRAYER

Truth: We can ask God to help us share.

Teach children to clap as they say this sharing prayer before free play or learning center time. You may also want to use it as a gentle intervention when children argue over a toy.

Thank you, God, that we have fun
With teachers, friends, and everyone.
Help us always to obey
And share our toys each time we play.

GROWING BODY PRAYER

Truth: We can thank God for our growing bodies.

Preschoolers are fascinated by their growing bodies. And sometimes those little bodies need to move! Use this action prayer when your little ones need to get the wiggles out. You may want to repeat it two or three times, going a little faster each time.

Thank you for my fingers. *(Wiggle fingers.)*
Thank you for my toes. *(Touch toes.)*
Thank you for my two strong legs *(jump up and down),*
And for my hair that grows. *(Put hands on head.)*
Thank you for my eyes that blink *(point to eyes and blink),*
And for my happy smile. *(Point to mouth and smile.)*
Thank you, God, for all of me! *(Stretch arms wide.)*
I'm glad to be your child. *(Hug yourself.)*

Out of the Ordinary!

"In all my prayers for all of you, I always pray with joy" (Philippians 1:4, NIV).

While a young mother named Molly attended a Bible study on Isaiah, her son attended an age-appropriate lesson for children on the same topic. As Christmas drew near, Molly appreciated for the first time how many prophecies had been fulfilled by Jesus' birth. Wanting to share these insights with her family, she invited them to pray around their ceramic crèche scene. Suddenly her son blurted out, "You can't make me pray to stone idols!"

There are an infinite number of prayer variations. Sometimes prayer is poignant and beautiful. Sometimes prayer is boisterous and noisy. But prayer always brings to us a better understanding of God and a closer relationship with the Mighty Creator.

Break out of the ordinary routine of prayer with these exciting prayer ideas that will help you turn an everyday class into an incredible event! At the same time, you'll be teaching kids that communicating with God is not confined to specific times, words, or places. These creative prayer ideas for every learning style will help your kids discover that prayer is an adventure.

SILENT PRAYER WALK
Truth: God wants us to pray for strangers and friends.

Use this idea with middle to older elementary kids.

Say: **We're going on a silent prayer walk. We won't talk to each other or to anyone we meet. I'll give hand signals to tell you when to go, stop, or turn. As we walk, we'll see individuals or groups of people. Silently pick out the people you'd like to pray for, and pray as you walk by them. After we return to our class, we'll talk about our experiences. Once we step out of this room, there'll be no talking until we return and I tell you it's OK to talk. Let's go!**

Lead kids around the neighborhood that surrounds your church. Gauge the length of your walk according to your kids' attention span. When you return to your room, ask:

● **What kinds of feelings did you experience during our prayer walk?**
● **What did you learn from praying this way?**
● **How did our prayer walk change the way you look at people?**

Close by praying: **Lord, thank you for the privilege of praying for people. Thank you for loving each person—friend or stranger—we prayed for today. Help us keep seeing people through your eyes. In Jesus' name, amen.**

Extra Idea! Do a similar prayer walk within the walls of your church. Pause beside each room where people are meeting, and pray for those people. Visit the pastor's study, and pray for him. Stand in the pulpit area, and pray for people who lead your services. Pray around the musical instruments. You may want to leave little notes in each location that say, "(Name of your class) prayed for you today. God bless you!"

⊚DOUGHN'T YOU LOVE TO PRAY?

Truth: God has answered our prayers before, and God will answer our prayers today.

You'll need a mixing bowl, peanut butter, powdered sugar, wax paper, and napkins. You may want to play a recording of soft worship music to help kids focus on prayer.

Make peanut butter dough by mixing approximately equal parts of peanut butter and powdered sugar. Knead in sugar until the dough is smooth and not too sticky. Have kids form trios. Give each trio three napkins and a lump of dough on a sheet of wax paper.

Say: **Divide your dough into three parts, and give each person a lump of dough. Use your dough to model something that represents the answer to prayer that's been really important to you. Please work quietly. When you've finished, place your dough model on the wax paper, and set it on the floor in front of you.**

When most kids have finished, give a thirty-second warning. Then call time, and invite kids to tell their trio members about the answers to prayer they modeled. Allow a minute or two for sharing; then ask a volunteer to offer a prayer of thanks to God for answered prayer.

Then say: **Now please use your dough to model something that represents a prayer concern you have right now. Work quietly, and set your dough model on your napkin when you've finished.**

CHAPTER FIVE

Hooray! Let's Pray! ● Hooray! Let's Pray! ● Hooray! Let's Pray!

STICKY PRAYERS

Truth: Thank God for good friends.

You'll need self-stick notes and pencils. (If you have young nonwriters in your group, form pairs and give each younger child an older partner.)

Gather kids in a circle, and give each person as many self-stick notes as there are kids in your class. Have each child write the name of one classmate at the top of each note. Beneath the name, have each child write a simple prayer for that person. When kids have finished writing, have them stick their prayer notes on the appropriate people. (This causes a happy jumble of kids!) Close by thanking God for each child and for the friendships God has given.

Extra Idea! Have kids prepare sticky-note prayers for your pastor or for another church leader. Then delight him or her with a "prayer ambush" by having kids surround the happy "victim" and stick on their prayer notes.

ONE-WORD PRAYERS

Truth: God understands our hearts even when we pray a single word.

Use this simple prayer idea to help kids become accustomed to praying out loud.

Gather kids in a circle and say: **We're going to pray together in a very unique way. Each person will say just one word. No one else has to understand your word—it's just between you and God. You might say the name of a person, you might say a word that tells how you're feeling, or you might just say, "Thank you." I'll begin; then we'll go around the circle. When we get all the way around the circle, I'll say "amen."**

Extra Idea! The one-word prayer also works well on a poster. Set out colored markers. Let kids write their words in plain or fancy letters. Hang the prayer poster on a wall, and let kids add to it whenever they wish.

CHAPTER FIVE

Hooray! Let's Pray! ● Hooray! Let's Pray! ● Hooray! Let's Pray!

IN-THE-NEWS PRAYERS

Truth: We can search out and pray for people in need.

Set out several recent newspapers. Let kids scan the newspapers for stories of people in need. After each child has chosen an article, gather kids in a circle and invite them to tell about their stories. After each person shares his or her story, invite that person to pray for the people in the story.

Extra Idea! Use a video-prayer format to record a television newscast. Between each story, pause the video and ask a volunteer to pray for that situation.

A TO Z POP-UP PRAISES

Truth: God is greatly to be praised.

Say: **We're going to offer God a prayer of praise by calling out praise words that begin with each letter of the alphabet. For example, when I call out the letter A, you might think of the word, "amazing." You'd pop up out of your chair, shout that word, and then pop back down again.**

Call out the letters of the alphabet, pausing for a few seconds after each one. (When you come to X, allow "ex" words, such as "exciting" and "excellent.")

ALLELUIA AMBLE

Truth: Everything we see can remind us to pray.

Use this prayer with middle and older elementary kids. Form groups of six, and assign an adult leader to each group.

Say: **We're going to take a walk and talk to God about the things we notice. For instance, if you see a road sign, you might pray, "Thank you, God, that you are the way, the truth, and the life." If you see a pine tree, you might pray, "Lord, you made the pine tree prickly. I've been prickly lately. Please forgive me and help me be more loving." If you see a telephone wire, you might pray, "Lord, I'm glad that I can call on you in prayer any**

CHAPTER FIVE

Hooray! Let's Pray! ● Hooray! Let's Pray! ● Hooray! Let's Pray!

time and that you never give me a busy signal." Pray out loud so the members of your group can join in your prayers.

Take the kids on a walk, and begin the prayer by praising God for something you see. Encourage the children to join in and make prayer connections with things they see. After a few minutes, lead the group back to the room, and pray: **God, we thank you for creating our world with so many things that remind us of you and what you do for us. You are truly a great God. Amen.**

HOUSEHOLD HALLELUJAHS

Truth: Everyday items can help us pray.

Set out on a tray household items such as a fingernail file, a blunt knife, a pen, an eraser, a spoon, scissors, a bar of soap, a flashlight or candle, a crayon, a cookie cutter, a spatula, and salt and pepper shakers. Form pairs, and have kids sit in a circle with their partners. Say: **In just a moment I'm going to pass this tray around. Each pair can take an item and use it as a prayer starter. For instance, if you choose the flashlight, you might pray, "Jesus, thank you for being the light of the world."**

After pairs have chosen their items, walk around the circle and offer suggestions as needed. When everyone has a prayer idea, pass the tray around the circle again. Have each pair offer its prayer and then place its item back on the tray and pass the tray to the next pair.

Encourage kids to use this prayer idea with their families.

ROCKIN' AND TALKIN' TO GOD

Truth: Our praise and thanks can be songs to God.

Kids will love singing this mealtime or snack time grace to the tune of "Rock Around the Clock."

God is great; God is good.
And we thank him for our food.
We're gonna thank him in the morning, noon, and night.

We're gonna thank him 'cuz he's out of sight.
We're thankin' our God morning, noon, and night.
Amen. Amen. Amen.

HUNGRY JAWS

Truth: Thanking God can be fun.

Sing this prayer in the growly two-beat rhythm of the theme song of the movie, *Jaws*. Begin by having kids put their hands together over their heads like fins. On "amen," have kids spread their arms like huge jaws and then snap them shut.

God-is	great-and	God-is	good-and
So-we	thank-him	for-our	fo-od.
Aaaaa-men!			

HOKEY POKEY PRAYERS

Truth: Prayer is about praising, thanking, and loving God.

This is a great way to introduce prayer at a lively, large group gathering. Sing it to the tune of the "Hokey Pokey" and do the motions indicated in the song.

Put your prayin' hands in.
Put your prayin' hands out.
Raise them up to heaven,
And shake them all about.
Give your praise to Jesus
As you twist and shout.
That's what prayin's all about.

Put your prayin' hands in.
Put your prayin' hands out.
Raise them up to heaven,
And shake them all about.
Give your praise to Jesus

CHAPTER FIVE

Hooray! Let's Pray! ● Hooray! Let's Pray! ● Hooray! Let's Pray!

As you twist and shout.
That's what prayin's all about.

Put your prayin' hands in.
Put your prayin' hands out.
Raise them up to heaven,
And shake them all about.
Give your praise to Jesus
As you twist and shout.
That's what prayin's all about.

A PARTING PRAYER

Truth: God takes care of us when we part from each other.

Sing this prayer-benediction to the tune of "Edelweiss."

Thank you, Lord, mighty Lord,
For each one in this place,
For your love that makes us one
And holds us together in grace.

Be with us here and with friends far and near.
We pray for each sister and brother.
Keep us all in your love
As we part from each other.

MUSICAL ADORATION

Truth: Prayer is adoration.

Use the chorus of the Christmas carol, "O Come All Ye Faithful" to set the mood for prayer at any children's gathering.

O come, let us adore him.
O come, let us adore him.
O come, let us adore him,
Christ the Lord!

TEAR A PRAYER

Truth: We can pray all kinds of prayers.

You'll need a Bible and office paper—paper that's been used on one side will work great. You may want to play soft, meditative music. Gather kids in a circle and read Ephesians 6:18 aloud.

Say: **This verse invites us to pray all kinds of prayers. So today we're going to tear our prayers.**

Give each child three sheets of paper. Say: **Think about a situation your family has been concerned about. It might be that someone in your family needs a job, that someone is in a difficult relationship, or that money is tight. Tear your paper into a shape that represents your concern. No one else needs to know what your shape stands for. As you tear your paper, pray for God to take care of that concern.**

As kids work, make a torn-paper prayer of your own. After about a minute, say: **Place your torn-paper prayer behind you, and pick up another sheet of paper. This time tear a shape that represents something that brings you joy. It might be a pet, a favorite book, or a special friendship. As you tear a prayer, thank God for the joy you feel.**

Again, allow about a minute for kids to tear and pray. Then say: **Place that paper behind you, and pick up your last sheet of paper. Think about someone you don't get along with— someone who's been mean to you, or someone you don't like. Please tear a heart shape from your paper. As you tear a prayer, ask God to help you love that difficult person.**

Encourage kids to keep their torn-paper prayers and to add to them to create unique prayer journals.

CANDLELIGHT PRAISES

Truth: Prayer is offering a sacrifice of praise.

You'll need a Bible, matches, a pillar candle, and small, individual candles with paper collars to protect kids' hands from dripping wax.

Place the pillar candle on a table in the center of a darkened room. As you light the candle, invite kids to gather in a circle around the table.

Stand by the candle and say: **Today we're going to offer prayers of praise in a different way. In Old Testament times, people gave burnt offerings and sacrifices to God.** Read Hebrews 13:15 aloud; then continue: **As Hebrews 13:15 explains, instead of giving offerings of animals or grain, our sacrifices to God are our praises. The psalm I'm about to read is your invitation to praise God by telling about the wonderful things God has done.**

Read Psalm 66:1-5. Then pick up a small candle, light it from the pillar candle, and complete this sentence prayer: **God, I praise you for** _____. Invite kids to take candles and follow your example.

When everyone has prayed and lit a candle, say: **The Bible describes many instances when God's glory shone in the temple, in heaven, and even on the faces of people. For example, listen to Luke 2:9.** Read Luke 2:9. Say: **Our room is glowing because we've given God glory for the wonderful things he's done.**

Have everyone carefully extinguish the candles. You may want to allow kids to take their candles home to use during personal quiet times with God. If you do, encourage children to get their parents' permission and to ask for a safe candleholder.

BREAKING BREAD

Truth: We thank Jesus for forgiveness, peace, and love.

You'll need a loaf of shepherd's bread or French bread. This experience of prayer and fellowship is an ancient custom among Christians that may be totally new to your students.

Gather kids in a circle and say: **In Bible times, breaking bread and eating together held special significance. People broke bread together to seal an agreement, and as a symbol of peace, friendship, and goodwill.**

Break off portions of bread and hand one to each student. Say: **Today we're going to break bread together to show that we love and forgive each other as brothers and sisters in Christ. Break off a piece of your bread, and eat it as I pray.**

Pray: **Jesus, we thank you for your sacrifice that cleansed our sins and made our peace with God. We ask that you help us forgive each other and live in peace.**

Pause for a few moments, then say: **Now to "pass the peace." I'll**

CHAPTER FIVE

Hooray! Let's Pray! ● Hooray! Let's Pray! ● Hooray! Let's Pray!

show you how to do that. Stand in front of a student, hand him or her a small piece of your bread, and say: **The peace of Jesus Christ be with you.** Prompt the student to give you a piece of his or her bread and respond, "And also with you."

Say: **Many churches use this prayerful experience to reaffirm friendships and to break down walls of anger and resentment between people. Please break bread and pass the peace with everyone in the class. Please do this quietly and respectfully. We are in God's presence and we're asking God to bless us with peace.**

Move among the children and coach them as necessary as they pass the peace. When everyone has finished, say: **Let's close by thanking God for being with us.**

Pray: **Dear Lord, thank you for honoring us with your presence. Please fill us with your peace and with love for each other. In Jesus' name, amen.**

Note: You may want to invite your pastor to your class to explain your church's doctrine on the Lord's Supper.

FREE INDEED

Truth: We thank God for setting us free from sin.

You'll need a large roll of string.

Say: **At some point, all of us have done something that was unfair, mean, rotten, downright despicable, or even a little bit wrong. Let's find out what happens to us when we do wrong things.**

Choose one child and say: **Hold your arms straight down at your sides. While I wrap this string around you, I want you to think of one wrong thing that you've done.** Encircle that child with string; then continue with the other kids. As you wrap the kids together, turn them in a tight circle to form a "large snail." For good measure, wrap the string two or three times around the whole snail. Hold the end of the string.

Then say: **It looks like you're all tangled up by the wrong things you've done. That happens to all of us. But there is a solution! Listen to what Jesus said.** Read John 8:34-36 aloud. Then ask:

● **How can we be set free from our sins?**

Say: **Jesus' love and forgiveness can set us free from our sins. All we have to do is ask. On the count of three, shout, "Jesus, set**

CHAPTER FIVE

Hooray! Let's Pray! ● Hooray! Let's Pray! ● Hooray! Let's Pray!

me free!" **Then you can spin around and unwind yourselves.**
As children unwind, have them help you gather all the discarded string into a big knot. Hold the knot of string as you close with prayer thanking Jesus for the wonderful freedom from sin he offers us.

PRAISES IN BLOOM
Truth: God cares for flowers, and we thank him for caring for us.

Bring a bouquet of flowers to class. Gather kids in a circle and set the bouquet in the middle. Ask:
● **What is your favorite kind of flower?**
● **What do flowers make you think of?**
Say: **Once Jesus was teaching a group of followers. As he looked out across the hillside, fields of beautiful wildflowers caught his eye. The flowers made him think of something. Listen to what he said.**
Read Luke 12:27-31 aloud. Then ask:
● **What did the flowers make Jesus think of?**
Say: **We're going to use this bouquet of flowers to thank God for the way he takes care of us.** Pull a flower from the bouquet and complete this sentence prayer: **Lord, I thank you for taking care of me by_____.** Invite kids to offer sentence prayers as they each take a flower. Encourage them to name things such as, "giving me a warm house," "giving me good friends," and "giving me enough to eat."
Have kids tuck their flowers behind their ears or into their pockets. Say: **The next time you see flowers in bloom, remember God's promise to take care of you!**

Special Times, Special Places

"About midnight Paul and Silas were praying and singing songs to God as the other prisoners listened" (Acts 16:25).

A preschool child drew a picture of the nativity with a large rolypoly person standing near baby Jesus. When asked who that was, the child responded, "That's Round John Virgin!"

We celebrate holidays and happy times with special food and decorations—now you can lead your students in celebrating with special prayers! This chapter offers prayer ideas for seasons, holidays, and special occasions as well as times of grief and loss. Use these prayers to help kids cope with difficult events and celebrate happy ones.

TREE-MENDOUS APPLAUSE!

Truth: Our prayers can celebrate God's goodness.

When fall has "fallen" and there are a lot of bright, crunchy leaves on the ground, gather kids in a leafy area such as a park. (If you live in an area without many deciduous trees, let kids make "leaves" by tearing and crumpling newspaper.)

Read aloud Isaiah 55:12 and explain that the verse means we can celebrate because God is so good. Tell kids that you're going to pray and help the trees "clap their hands" by applauding God's goodness. Start your prayer by saying, **"Dear God, we love you. You are** _____." Finish your sentence by saying a word or phrase that describes God, such as kind, powerful, merciful, amazing, or beautiful.

Then stomp on your pile of leaves to make a crunching "applause." Have kids take turns adding words, and then stomping the leaves. (The faster kids go, the more this sounds like applause!) Continue until everyone has had a turn or kids run out of ideas. Then jump into a pile of leaves and shout: **Amen!**

CHAPTER SIX

Hooray! Let's Pray! ● Hooray! Let's Pray! ● Hooray! Let's Pray!

HORNS OF PLENTY PRAYERS

Truth: Our prayers show our thankfulness.

Use this prayer as part of a Thanksgiving celebration. Place bowls of peanuts, M&M's candies, candy corn, raisins, and chocolate chips on a long table. Scatter spoons around the table. Place a stack of pointed ice cream cones at both ends of the table. Have kids form pairs.

Say: **At Thanksgiving time, lots of the decorations we see show cornucopias, sometimes called horns of plenty. They're brimming with vegetables and fruit from a good harvest. Today we're going to celebrate the "harvest" of good things God has done for us this year.**

The ice cream cones will be your horns of plenty. Travel around the table with your partner and stop in front of each bowl. Say, "I thank God for_____" and then finish the sentence by naming a good thing God has done for you this year. You might mention something good that's happened to your family, or a sick friend or relative who got well. Maybe you just want to thank God for our country or our church.

After you've shared what you're thankful for, you can each put a spoonful of goodies into your partner's horn of plenty and then move on to the next bowl.

After kids have shared their thanks and filled their horns of plenty, sing "Give Thanks." Then let kids enjoy their treats.

TURKEY TAIL THANKS

Truth: Giving thanks is fun.

On a large sheet of poster board, draw a simple turkey outline without the tail feathers, using the illustration as a guide. Cut tail feathers from construction paper in bright, autumn colors.

Set out the tail feathers and markers. Invite kids to draw or write the things they're most thankful for from the last twelve months. Have kids attach pieces of folded tape to the back of their feathers and share their thanks with the class. Blindfold kids one at a time, spin them around, and have them attach their feathers to the first thing they run into!

CHAPTER SIX

Hooray! Let's Pray! ● Hooray! Let's Pray! ● Hooray! Let's Pray!

After everyone has shared, pray a prayer of thanks together; then let the kids rearrange their feathers on the turkey.

CHRISTMAS CRADLE PRAYERS

Truth: Prayer can lead us to acts of service.

Make a manger from a wooden or cardboard box. Fill it with hay or shredded paper.

On the first Sunday of Advent, gather kids around the empty manger. Talk about what people do to get ready when a baby is about to be born. Ask kids to bring a small baby gift each week until Christmas. Suggest small items such as pacifiers, knit booties, bibs, rattles, bottles, or cans of formula.

Let children lay their gifts in the manger each week. Seeing familiar baby items will help kids grasp the reality of Jesus' birth. Each week ask a different child to pray and thank Jesus for coming to the earth as a baby. On the Sunday before Christmas, pack all the baby items in a box, and have the kids wrap and decorate it.

Take the box to a local shelter. If possible, have the children go with you when you make the special delivery.

ADVENT PRAYERS

Truth: Prayer prepares us for Christmastime.

Wrap the figures from a crèche scene and bring them to class in a box. Let each child pull out one or two figures without peeking to see what they are.

Let kids take turns unwrapping figures. As they add the figures to the crèche scene, have them give thanks for the role that figure played in Jesus' birth. For instance, the person holding the stable might say, "Thank you that there was at least a stable nearby where Jesus could be born." The person with a shepherd might say, "Thank you that the shepherds went and told lots of people about Jesus' birth."

After all the kids have added their figures and prayed, talk about the role we can all play in preparing for Jesus' birth and in telling people why Jesus came to earth. Close with a prayer asking God to help everyone be a faithful witness.

CHAPTER SIX

Hooray! Let's Pray! ● Hooray! Let's Pray! ● Hooray! Let's Pray!

⊚ CHRISTMAS QUIET

Truth: It is good to pray in silence and stillness.

You'll need three cassette or CD players and three cassettes or CDs of different styles of Christmas music. You'll also need index cards, pencils, and a figure of baby Jesus from a crèche scene.

Have kids sit in a circle. Place the three cassette or CD players around the edge of the circle. Pass out index cards and pencils, and invite kids to make lists of what they'd like to get for Christmas. As kids begin to write, play Christmas music on all three cassette or CD players with the volume turned as loud as your classroom location will permit.

After about a minute, stop the music, and have kids place their lists and pencils behind them. As you place the figure of baby Jesus in the center of the circle, say: **I'd like everyone to be perfectly silent for the next two minutes. You may close your eyes or look at this figure of baby Jesus, but please don't look at each other until I call time. During this quiet time, please pray and ask God to show you what's important about this Christmas season.**

After two minutes call time and ask:
● **What is important about this season?**
● **How was the noise from the cassette or CD players like what happens at Christmastime?**
● **What have you learned from this experience?**

Pray: **Dear Lord, it's so easy to be caught up in noise and confusion and busyness. Help us find time to be quiet this season and to be thankful that you came to earth to be our Savior. Amen.**

⊚ A CLEAN SLATE

Truth: When we pray for forgiveness, God cleanses our hearts.

You'll need colored glass ball Christmas ornaments and coarse salt.

Use this prayer as part of a New Year's celebration with middle to older elementary kids. Give each a solid colored glass ball Christmas ornament. (You can usually find these very inexpensively after Christmas.) Demonstrate how to carefully pull the wire loop and its base from the top of an ornament. Then have each child pour a spoonful of coarse salt into his or her ornament and cover the open top with a thumb. If the edges of the ornaments

CHAPTER SIX

Hooray! Let's Pray! ● Hooray! Let's Pray! ● Hooray! Let's Pray!

are sharp, cover the openings with tape.

Explain that when we pray and confess our sins, God takes those sins away and makes our hearts new and clean. Have children close their eyes and pray silently, asking God to forgive their wrong-doings. As kids pray, have them shake their ornaments vigorously so the salt rubs against the inside. After a minute, say "amen" and have kids look at their ornaments. The salt will have rubbed off much of the shiny paint, revealing a clear glass ball! (Some kids may need to shake the ornament a bit more to remove all of the paint.)

Let kids pour out the salt and then rinse and dry their orna-ments. Children can hang their clear ornaments as reminders to "keep their hearts clean" during the new year.

Extra Idea! Set out puffy paints and glitter glue and allow kids to decorate their New Year's ornaments. Encourage children to write a verse such as 1 John 1:9 as a reminder of God's forgiveness.

VALENTINE PRAYERS FROM THE HEART

Truth: Prayer is a way to express our love for others.

You'll need envelopes, scissors, markers, a paper punch, rib-bon, and bowls of assorted Valentine candies.

Have kids form pairs. Give each pair an envelope and scissors. Demonstrate how to cut heart pockets from the bottom corners of an envelope. Use the illustration as a guide. Let kids decorate their heart pockets with markers. Help each pair punch holes in the top of their heart pockets and thread lengths of ribbon through the holes to form hang-ers. Gather kids around bowls of Valentine candies.

Say: **As we fill our heart pockets with goodies, we're going to thank God for the wonder-ful people he's placed in our lives. I'm going to describe different kinds of people. I'd like you to share with your part-ner and with God the name of someone in your life who is like the person I describe.**

CHAPTER SIX

Hooray! Let's Pray! ● Hooray! Let's Pray! ● Hooray! Let's Pray!

Say, "Thank you, Lord, for_____," and finish the sentence with that person's name. After you've swapped names, you can put one piece of candy in each other's heart pockets.

Read this list of people, pausing after each description for kids to share names:

- **a special friend who's fun to be with**
- **someone who is a good listener and understands you**
- **someone who takes care of you when you're sick**
- **someone who gives you what you need and watches over you**
- **someone who cheers you up when you're sad**
- **someone who loves you no matter what**
- **someone who is special to you but lives far away**
- **someone who teaches you things you like to learn**

Close with a prayer similar to this one: **Lord, thank you so much for the loving people you bring into our lives. And thank you for the people who aren't so easy to love. Help us give lots of love in return. In Jesus' name, amen.**

PRAYERS ON A CROSS

Truth: We thank Jesus for his love, which makes ugly things beautiful.

You'll need squares of colorful tissue paper, silk flowers, and a simple cross made from scrap lumber. Attach U-shaped brads to the cross or cover it in chicken wire.

Gather children in a circle. Hold up the cross, and say: **There's nothing beautiful about a cross. The Romans used it to execute their worst criminals. But Jesus turned the cross into a beautiful thing when he gave his life for the sins of the world. We're going to turn this cross into a beautiful thing with our prayers. You may take turns adding flowers and tissue paper to the cross. Each time you add something, pray, "Thank you, Jesus, for your love."**

Let kids decorate the cross. Gather kids around the finished cross, and pray: **Thank you for turning the ugly cross into something beautiful. Help our lives to be beautiful as we live in your love. Amen.**

CHAPTER SIX

Hooray! Let's Pray! ● Hooray! Let's Pray! ● Hooray! Let's Pray!

⊚ EASTER EGG PRAYERS

Truth: We can thank God for the sacrifice of his Son and for the hope of the Resurrection.

Before class, use a permanent marker to label seven plastic eggs with the numbers one through seven. Place the following items in the eggs:
1. a small square of bread;
2. a grape;
3. a piece of purple cloth;
4. a thorn;
5. a piece of a leather shoelace;
6. a cross; and
7. a stone.

Hide the eggs around the room. Tell kids that you're going to have an Easter egg prayer hunt. Let kids hunt until they've found all seven eggs; then gather everyone in a circle, and have kids take turns opening the eggs in order.

After each egg is opened, have kids combine their knowledge of the Easter story to tell the significance of that item. Then have a volunteer pray a prayer of thanks for that part of the Easter story. For instance, a prayer for the bread might be, "Thank you, Lord, that you are the bread of life. Thank you that you let your body be broken for us."

If your children are very young or not familiar with the Easter story, tell about the items and offer thanks for them yourself.

⊚ STARS AND STRIPES

Truth: We can thank God for our country.

Use this prayer idea on a patriotic holiday.

Form a circle and place a sheet of newsprint in the middle, then set out silver star stickers and red markers. Use a blue marker and color a rectangle in the upper left corner so the newsprint resembles an American flag.*

Ask kids to share concerns they have about their country, such as pollution, wisdom for leaders, homelessness, disease, and crime. Encourage kids to think of specific concerns they have regarding your community. Have children take turns praying, "God, thank you for our country. Thank you for _____." Kids can finish their prayers with statements such as "our leaders," "allowing us to worship you

CHAPTER SIX

Hooray! Let's Pray! ● Hooray! Let's Pray! ● Hooray! Let's Pray!

freely," or "the freedoms we enjoy." Each time a child prays, have him or her add a star sticker to the blue section of the newsprint.

Then have children take turns praying, "God help us _____." Kids can finish their prayers with statements such as "elect Christian leaders," "stop polluting your creation," or "love others, instead of fighting all the time." Each time a child prays, have him or her add a red stripe across the newsprint. When your "flag" is complete, join hands around it and say "amen."

*Note: If you live in Canada, adapt this activity by drawing an outline of a large maple leaf on a piece of white shelf paper. As the children contribute their prayers, have them color in the maple leaf with red markers.

Extra Idea! If fireworks are allowed in your area, do this prayer outside. After you've prayed, distribute sparklers and light them. Have kids call out praise phrases as they wave their sparklers and celebrate God!

CRISIS PRAYERS

Truth: Our prayers show that we have faith in God.

Use this prayer idea when kids have been affected by a crisis situation in your church, community, or nation. You'll need a Bible and a spray bottle filled with water.

Read Psalm 122:6 aloud. Say: **God cares about what happens to us, and God wants us to pray. The city of Jerusalem has been conquered and reconquered many times over thousands of years. God cares about what happens to Jerusalem just as he cares about what happens to our** (church, town, country).

Once there was a great crisis in the land of Israel. Because the people turned away from God, there had been no rain for three years. There was little food, and wells and streams had run dry. God sent the prophet Elijah to challenge the prophets of Baal—the fake God that most of the people worshiped. Let's read what happened at that showdown.

Read 1 Kings 18:20-39, 42b-45a. Ask:
● **What two things did Elijah pray for?**
● **What happened when Elijah prayed?**

Say: **Let's celebrate the rain that came when Elijah prayed!** Squirt water in the air over the heads of all the kids. Be sure to get yourself a little wet, too! Then put down the spray bottle, and ask:

● **Do you believe God still answers prayer? Why or why not?**
● **How can we pray about our crisis?**

Let several kids pray sentence prayers. Then close with a prayer similar to this one: **Dear Lord, We know that you see us and love us. We know that you care about what has happened. We pray that you will help us to have faith to believe that you will work things out for the best. In Jesus' name, amen.**

A PRAYER FOR GRIEVING

Truth: We can pray when we're sad, and God will heal our hurts.

If your class or someone in your class is grieving the death of a loved one, help them understand and accept their loss with this beautiful prayer.

Purchase a few flower bulbs, and get permission to plant them on your church property. If it isn't possible to plant the bulbs outside, ask your florist for instructions on how to force the bulbs indoors.

Have the class help you dig a small hole for the bulbs. As kids place the bulbs in the hole, encourage kids to talk about what they appreciated about the person who died, and what they will remember about him or her.

As kids pat the dirt in place over the bulbs, say: **We've buried these bulbs, but we know they'll bloom in the spring. Right now** (name) **is blooming in heaven, and someday we'll see** (him or her) **there.**

Join hands with the kids and close with a prayer similar to this one: **Dear Lord, thank you for** (name's) **life and for all the wonderful memories we have. We feel** (his or her) **loss very much, and ask that you would heal our hurt. Thank you for the hope of heaven. In Jesus' name, amen.**

Be sure to bring kids to see the bulbs when they bloom and to remind kids that their loved one is blooming in heaven.

Hooray! Let's Pray! ● Hooray! Let's Pray! ● Hooray! Let's Pray!

BIRTHDAY BLESSINGS
Truth: We can thank God on our birthdays.

On a child's birthday cake (or other dessert), place one candle for every year of his or her life. As you light each candle, have the child pray and thank God for one thing that happened in the past year.

Then have that child blow out the candles one by one, and pray for something in the future. Kids might pray, "Help Grandma learn about you," "Show me how to be kind to our next-door neighbor," or "Teach me to be helpful at home." When all the candles are blown out, join hands and thank God for this special member of your class.

Extra Idea! Give each child a cupcake with a candle in it. As you light the candles, have each person pray for the birthday boy or girl. Then have everyone blow out the candles.

FLOATING PRAYERS
Truth: God is with us even when we must part from one another.

If you've been camping near a river or a body of water with a current, you'll want to experience this extraordinarily beautiful prayer as a parting benediction.

You'll need tea light candles that aren't encased in metal. You'll also need small, flat pieces of wood, matches, and buckets of water.

Plan to do this after dark on an evening when the air is calm. Make sure you have plenty of adults on hand to keep children from getting too near the water. Place buckets of water on the shore downstream, just in case the candles float too close to the shoreline.

Gather children by the shore at a location where it's safe to approach the water. Say: **We're about to part from each other and go in different directions, but we know that the Lord goes with each of us. We'll take turns lighting candles and setting them afloat in the water. As each person pushes a candle into the current, pray that God will be with that person as he or she leaves.**

Help kids light their candles one by one, place the candle on a piece of wood, and push it gently into the current. Encourage everyone to be prayerful and quiet. The scene of lights on the water floating into the distance is unforgettable. Close the experience with a song such as "The Bond of Love."

CHAPTER SIX

Hooray! Let's Pray! ● Hooray! Let's Pray! ● Hooray! Let's Pray!

Note: Candle wax isn't toxic to wildlife. But if you're concerned about adding unnatural items to a natural water source, do this activity in a swimming pool or do it in the daytime and float natural items such as flowers.

CAMPFIRE PRAISE

Truth: Our praises rise to heaven and to God's ear.

Lead kids on a trek around the church grounds, and have them collect two twigs apiece. Than gather around a charcoal grill or fireplace for a special prayer. Explain that in biblical times, people lit incense and burned sacrifices to show their love for God. The sweet-smelling smoke rising into the sky represented the peoples' praises rising to heaven (Psalm 141:2; Revelation 8:3-4).

Lead kids in praising God by praying: **God, you are** _____, and finish the sentence with a one-word description of God. You might use words like powerful, compassionate, awesome, or amazing. Then toss a twig into the fire. Invite kids to express their one-word praises to God and toss their twigs into the fire.

When everyone has had a turn, pray: **God, help me to be** _____, and finish the sentence with a trait you'd like to develop, such as kindness, patience, or helpfulness. Add another twig to the fire, and continue around the circle. When everyone has prayed, join hands around the fire and say: **Amen.**

Extra Idea! Bring marshmallows, graham crackers, and chocolate bars to your "campfire." As kids roast their marshmallows, have them pray for people who are "in the fire" or going through difficult times. Then sandwich your toasted marshmallows between graham crackers and chocolate bars to make S'mores. Talk about how God sandwiches us with his love and peace when we pray.

A PRAYER FOR MOVING AWAY

Truth: We can ask for God to be with friends who move away.

Moving to a new town brings a great sense of loss, both to the child who is leaving and to the children who are left behind. Use this

CHAPTER SIX

Hooray! Let's Pray! ● Hooray! Let's Pray! ● Hooray! Let's Pray!

prayer to comfort kids when a friend moves on.

Photocopy onto colorful paper the "We'll Always Be Friends" handout (p. 70), and cut it out. Write in the name of the child who is leaving; then have the rest of the students add their autographs. Encourage kids to write their addresses as well. It's great if you can accomplish this on the sly so it's a surprise. When everyone is finished, fold the card and tape it shut.

Gather kids in a circle, and say to the child who's moving: **We're going to miss you. We have a card for you, and I'd like to read the promise that's inside.** Read Deuteronomy 31:8 from the card, then have kids form a tight huddle.

Pray: **Dear Lord, thank you for the wonderful gift of friendship. Thank you for your promise to be with** (name of child) **as he** (or she) **moves to a new place. Please help him** (or her) **to find friends and to be very happy there. Thank you that we can look forward to friendships in heaven that will never end. In Jesus' name, amen.**

HANDOUT

Hooray! Let's Pray! ● Hooray! Let's Pray! ● Hooray! Let's Pray!

We'll Always Be Friends

WE'LL ALWAYS BE FRIENDS.

"The Lord himself will go before you. He will be with you; he will not leave you or forget you. Don't be afraid and don't worry" (Deuteronomy 31:8).

Prayers From the Bible

"Be full of joy in the Lord always. I will say again, be full of joy. Let everyone see that you are gentle and kind. The Lord is coming soon. Do not worry about anything, but pray and ask God for everything you need, always giving thanks. And God's peace, which is so great we cannot understand it, will keep your hearts and minds in Christ Jesus" (Philippians 4:4-7).

A mother who stayed home from church with the flu asked her nine-year-old son to tell her about the sermon. "It had something to do with a quilt," was his cryptic reply. Questioning her husband later, the woman discovered that the pastor had preached on John 14:16: "And I will pray the Father, and he shall give you another Comforter" (King James Version).

Getting kids "into the Word" is always a challenge. The Bible is, after all, complex in structure and bewildering to young readers. These prayers from Scripture will help kids see God's Word in a whole new light. No doubt they'll be surprised to learn that many of their favorite praise songs and choruses come directly from Scripture. (Many of the Scripture songs listed in this chapter can be found in *The Group Songbook* (available from Group Publishing). Use these prayer ideas to help kids realize how important, exciting, and relevant the Bible can be.

EXODUS 15:1

Truth: Prayer can be happy and noisy.

This happy prayer of praise is the basis of the song "I Will Sing Unto the Lord (The Horse and Rider)," number 54 in *The Group Songbook*.

Let kids sing this prayer and use a variety of pots, pans, wooden spoons, rhythm instruments, and other noisemakers for accompaniment.

Younger children will enjoy galloping as they sing. Older children will enjoy developing complicated clapping rhythms for the chorus.

⟳PSALM 8
Truth: God is majestic.

Let kids sing this prayer along with a CD or cassette recording of "How Majestic Is Your Name" by Michael W. Smith. The song is number 71 in *The Group Songbook.*

Have the children crouch down to begin the song and jump up on the word "majestic." Have them flutter their hands overhead on the word "praise" and hold an imaginary magnifying glass to their eyes on the word "magnify."

⟳PSALM 23
Truth: God is our shepherd.

Teach kids to read Psalm 23 as a prayer by inserting "you" in place of "he" when it refers to God. Begin the psalm, "Lord, you are my shepherd."

Younger children will enjoy pretending to be sheep. Play the part of the shepherd, and round them up. Pretend to lead them to cool water and green grass.

Older children will enjoy coming up with creative motions to go with the psalm.

⟳PSALM 42
Truth: Our prayers express our devotion to God.

This psalm inspired the song, "As the Deer," number 34 in *The Group Songbook.* Invite kids to sing this prayer-song with a quiet accompaniment.

With older children, try eating salty food such as popcorn or pretzels before singing this song. Read Psalm 42:1 from the New International Version. Put a large pitcher of ice water in the middle of the room, and gather the children around it while you sing. After the song, pour each child a tall glass of refreshing, cold water, and encourage a discussion on the ways that God refreshes us.

Extra Idea: Have the children write similes that express their longing for God. Have them finish this sentence: "My soul longs for you like the _____." To get them started, suggest that they make a list of

CHAPTER SEVEN

Hooray! Let's Pray! ● Hooray! Let's Pray! ● Hooray! Let's Pray!

descriptive, personal nouns, such as poet or soldier. Then have them consider what those people might long for. Then have them complete the sentence: "My soul longs for you like the poet who seeks a rhyme," or "My soul longs for you like the soldier who longs for peace."

PSALM 51

Truth: We can thank God for washing our sins away.

You'll need a Bible, newspapers, a towel, and a dishpan of warm, fragrant soapy water or access to a sink and hand soap.

Hand each child a sheet of newspaper. Say: **As you rub your hands with the newspaper, think of wrong things you have done.** Pause as kids do this. Their hands will become dirty from the newspaper ink. Then say: **As I read this psalm, close your eyes, and make it your prayer.**

Read Psalm 51:1-12 aloud. Then allow kids to wash and dry their hands. Gather the group in a circle, and pray: **Thank you, Lord, for taking our sins away and making us cleaner than snow. In Jesus' name, amen.**

You may want to teach kids the song, "Create in Me a Clean Heart," number 36 in *The Group Songbook*.

PSALM 97:9

Truth: Prayer is a way to lift God's name above the earth.

You'll need a simple kite and a breezy day. You may want to have the children each make or bring his or her own kite to fly.

Take the kids outside and fly the kites. Once the kites are in the air, lead kids in singing the prayer-song "I Exalt Thee," number 39 in *The Group Songbook*.

Talk about what each line of the song means. Ask:

● **What does it mean when we say, "For thou, O Lord, art high above all the earth"?**

● **What does it mean when we sing, "Thou art exalted far above all gods"?**

● **What does it mean when we sing, "I exalt thee"?**

After your discussion, have the children watch the kites and prayerfully sing the song again.

CHAPTER SEVEN

Hooray! Let's Pray! ● Hooray! Let's Pray! ● Hooray! Let's Pray!

PSALM 100:4

Truth: Praise and thanksgiving are fun.

Sing this psalm as a prayer by changing "his" to "your." "I Will Enter His Gates" is number 87 in *The Group Songbook*.

Have the children use their feet and hands to stomp and clap their praise to God.

PSALM 136

Truth: God's love lasts forever.

This psalm/prayer is great fun to do with a speaking group and a singing group. The speaking group reads the first line of each verse. The singing group responds with a jazzy chant, "Ooh ooh ooh ooh. For his love endures forever." Use the music below for the chant, or let your kids create a rap beat of their own.

Ooh ooh ooh ooh. For His love en-dures for-ev-er.

JONAH 2:1-10

Truth: God's forgiveness frees us.

You'll need a Bible and a large paper grocery bag for each child. Have the children sit down while you briefly review the story of Jonah, or read it directly from the Bible. When Jonah gets swallowed by the fish, have kids put the paper bags over their heads. Be sensitive to children who don't want to put the bags over their heads—have them close their eyes instead.

Say: **You're inside the fish with Jonah, and you're thinking about times you've disobeyed God. When I read that the fish spits Jonah out, throw the bags off your heads, and jump up and cheer.**

Read Jonah 2:1-10. After the kids have thrown off their bags and cheered, gather them in a huddle and pray: **Lord, sometimes we**

Hooray! Let's Pray! ● Hooray! Let's Pray! ● Hooray! Let's Pray!

get swallowed up by the bad things we do and by our disobe-
dience to you. Thank you for hearing and answering our
prayers for forgiveness. In Jesus' name, amen.

⊚ MATTHEW 6:33 AND 7:7

Truth: Prayer is a way to commit ourselves to God.

Modify the words of the song "Seek Ye First" (number 67 in
The Group Songbook) to sing these verses as a prayer.
I will seek first your kingdom, O God,
And your righteousness.
I pray, Lord, that you will provide the things I need.
Hall-le-lu, hal-le-lu-jah.

Lord, when I ask, I pray that you will give;
I'll seek your will every day,
And when I knock, please open a way.
Hall-le-lu, hal-le-lu-jah.

⊚ MATTHEW 5:44

Truth: We can pray for our enemies.

You'll need Bibles, thorny weeds, and lightweight jute twine.
Plan to play a CD or cassette of soft worship music in the background. Hand out Bibles, and have kids look up Matthew 5:44. Ask
a volunteer to read the verse aloud. Then say: **Praying for our
enemies is a lot harder than praying for people we love and
for things we want. But Jesus tells us specifically to do this.**
Start the music, then hand each child a thorny weed. Say: **Let
this thorn represent people you have a hard time getting
along with—people who aren't nice to you. As you pray, let
Jesus be your example. He prayed for God to forgive the
people who put him on the cross.**
Allow about a minute of silent prayer; then begin passing out
twelve-inch lengths of jute twine. Say: **Tie your weed in the middle of your twine. Then knot the ends of the twine together to
form a necklace. Hang the necklace somewhere in your room
as a reminder of Jesus' command to pray for our enemies.**

Hooray! Let's Pray! ● Hooray! Let's Pray! ● Hooray! Let's Pray!

THE LORD'S PRAYER

Truth: Jesus has given us a model for prayer.

Have kids open their Bibles to Matthew 6:9-13.

Say: **We're going to personalize this prayer that Jesus taught his disciples. As we read this prayer aloud, change the word "us" to "me," the word "our" to "my," and the word "we" to "I." We'll pause after each phrase. During the pause, you are free to personalize the prayer even more by praying for specific things. For example, when we ask God to forgive us, you can talk to God about the specific things you need forgiveness for. Let's pray.**

Lead the prayer. Pause after each phrase, and allow silent time for the children to talk to God.

THE LORD'S PRAYER
IN SIMPLE LANGUAGE

Truth: Prayer can be simple.

To help kids who aren't familiar with religious language learn and understand the Lord's Prayer, begin by teaching them this simplified version.

> Our Father,
> We know you live in heaven.
> Let people know how special you are.
> Come and be our King so that everyone will do what you want the way they do in heaven.
> Give us the food we need for today.
> Please forgive us for the wrong things we have done, and help us forgive people who do wrong things to us.
> Help us to not want to do wrong things and take care of us,
> Because you are the King who is powerful and great.
> Amen.

CHAPTER SEVEN

Hooray! Let's Pray! ● Hooray! Let's Pray! ● Hooray! Let's Pray!

⊚ 1 CORINTHIANS 12:12-13, 24, 27 AND JOHN 17:20-23

Truth: Prayer helps us stay connected to each other.

You'll need large rubber bands and a bag of wrapped candies, such as Hershey's Kisses.

Say: **The Apostle Paul said that God's people are the body of Christ, and that as parts of Christ's body, we all have different gifts and jobs to do. To show that we're all one body, let's form a circle and connect our wrists with rubber bands.** When kids are connected, read aloud 1 Corinthians 12:12-13. Then read verse 27 and verse 24. Then ask:

● **What does Paul say the different parts of the body should do for each other?**

Say: **We're going to care for each other by feeding each other a treat. Since we're all connected, we'll have to work together very carefully. I'd like each person to feed a treat to the person on his or her right.**

Pass the bag of candies. After each person has been fed, ask:

● **What did this experience teach you about being together in the body of Christ?**

Say: **At the Last Supper, Jesus prayed a special prayer for his disciples. He knew that he would not be with them for much longer, and he wanted them to stay together—to help each other and to stay true to their purpose. That's important for us, too. Please pray with me as I read Jesus' prayer.**

Read John 17:20-23 and close with: **Amen.**

⊚ GALATIANS 5:22-23

Truth: We can ask God to help us grow spiritually.

You'll need a large bowl; toothpicks; small paper plates, plastic knives, and several kinds of fruit such as grapes, bananas, cherries, canned mandarin orange segments and canned pineapple chunks.

Say: **The Bible tells us what our lives will be like when God's Spirit lives in us. Listen to what God's Spirit can do in our lives.** Read Galatians 5:22-23 aloud. Continue: **Today we're going to pray that our lives will be filled with the fruit of the Spirit. But before we pray, we need to make a fruit salad.**

Have kids wash their hands and help you cut up and assemble the fruit in a large bowl. Distribute plates and toothpicks, and gather

77

Hooray! Let's Pray! ● Hooray! Let's Pray! ● Hooray! Let's Pray!

kids around the bowl. Say: **I'm going to read Galatians 5:22-23 once more and pause after each "fruit" that's mentioned. I'll pray a sentence prayer and take a piece of fruit from the bowl and place it on my plate. Then you can take turns finishing the sentence prayer and taking fruit from the bowl. We'll wait until the end of our prayer time to eat the fruit.**

Read the Scripture passage again. Pause after each "fruit" and finish these sentence prayers.

Lord, help me be loving when...
Lord, help me be joyful when...
Lord, help me feel your peace when...
Lord, help me be patient when...
Lord, help me be kind when...
Lord, help me do good things when...
Lord, help me be faithful when...
Lord, help me be gentle when...
Lord, help me stay in control when...

Close the prayer time with a prayer similar to this one: **Thank you, Lord, for sending the Holy Spirit to work in our lives. Help us to be aware of your presence and to be open to your guidance. In Jesus' name, amen.**

Enjoy the fruit salad together.

◎ PRAYER BY THE SQUARE

Truth: We can pray for each other.

Kids will delight in constructing a game board of Scriptures about prayer and prayer instructions. Best of all, they'll review the Scriptures again and again and mature in their ability to pray for others!

Photocopy on colorful card stock the handouts "Prayer by the Square #1," "Prayer by the Square #2," and "Prayer by the Square Spinner" (pp. 80-82). Set out the handouts, scissors, large sheets of construction paper, glue sticks, paper fasteners, and sharpened pencils. You may want to make a sample game board before class.

Say: **Please take a paper fastener, a sheet of construction paper, and a copy of all three handouts. You're going to use them to make a Prayer by the Square game board.** If you made a sample game board, pass it around for kids to see.

Say: **First, cut apart all the squares on the handouts. Then arrange them in a twisting path on your construction paper. Once you're happy with your arrangement, glue them in place. After you've finished the game board, cut out the spinner and**

Hooray! Let's Pray! ● Hooray! Let's Pray! ● Hooray! Let's Pray!

arrow. **Use the point of a pencil to poke holes through the X's on the spinner and arrow; then put a paper fastener through the holes, fasten it in place, and you're ready to go!**

After kids have assembled their game boards, have them pair up to play and pray with partners. Instruct each pair to use one partner's game board for two or three minutes, then switch to the other partner's game board. Encourage kids to use the game boards to pray at home. Explain that they can pray alone or invite family members to join them.

BIRTHDAY BLESSING PRAYER

Truth: We pray for others on their birthdays.

Honor your birthday kids once a month with this special prayer composed of blessings from Scripture. For a special treat, you may want to make birthday crowns from poster board and foil. Make a "throne" by draping a quilt or crepe-paper garlands over a chair. Photocopy the "Birthday Blessing Verses" and the "Birthday Blessing Pocket" (pp. 83-84). Cut out and assemble the pocket and fill in the birthday child's name. Cut apart the blessing verses, and give each verse to a different child. Seat the birthday person on the throne and give him or her the Birthday Blessing Pocket.

Say: **We'd like to honor your birthday with a special blessing prayer.**

Have each child read his or her verse and then place the verse in the Birthday Blessing Pocket. Make sure the verses are read in numerical order. When the last verse has been read, place the crown on the child's head and say: **As a member of God's royal family, I crown you Prince** (or Princess) **(name). Happy birthday!**

Close with a prayer similar to this one: **Dear Lord, thank you for** (child's name). **Thank you for all the wonderful things you're going to do in his** (or her) **life this year. We pray that** (child's name) **will grow in you and feel your presence in his** (or her) **life every day. In Jesus' name, amen.**

Encourage the birthday person to keep the Birthday Blessings Pocket and to read the verses when he or she needs encouragement.

HANDOUT

Hooray! Let's Pray! ● Hooray! Let's Pray! ● Hooray! Let's Pray!

Prayer by the Square #1

"Our Father in heaven, may your name always be kept holy. May your kingdom come and what you want be done, here on earth as it is in heaven" (Matthew 6:9b-10).	Pray for homeless children.	"I say to you, love your enemies. Pray for those who hurt you. If you do this, you will be true children of your Father in heaven" (Matthew 5:44-45a).
Pray for someone who is sick.	"But I pray to you, Lord, for favor. God, because of your great love, answer me. You are truly able to save" (Psalm 69:13).	Pray for someone who doesn't know Jesus.
"Pray in the Spirit at all times with all kind of prayers, asking for everything you need. To do this you must always be ready and never give up. Always pray for all God's people" (Ephesians 6:18).	Pray for someone who's been mean to you.	"First, I tell you to pray for all people, asking God for what they need and being thankful to him" (1 Timothy 2:1).
Pray for the people in your family.	"I will praise you, Lord, with all my heart. I will tell all the miracles you have done. I will be happy because of you; God Most High, I will sing praises to your name" (Psalm 9:1-2).	Pray for leaders of our country.

Prayer by the Square #2

Pray for someone who is unhappy.	"Always be joyful. Pray continually, and give thanks for whatever happens" (1 Thessalonians 5:16-18a).	Pray that God will help you be a friend to someone who's lonely.
"Ask, and God will give to you. Search, and you will find. Knock, and the door will open for you" (Matthew 7:7).	Pray about something that's been worrying you.	"By helping each other with your troubles, you truly obey the law of Christ" (Galatians 6:2).
Pray for someone who needs a job.	"Give us the food we need for each day. Forgive us our sins, just as we have forgiven those who sinned against us" (Matthew 6:11-12).	Pray for a missionary in another country.
"My whole being, praise the Lord. Lord my God, you are very great. You are clothed with glory and majesty" (Psalm 104:1).	Pray for peace in countries that are at war.	"Do not worry about anything, but pray and ask God for everything you need, always giving thanks" (Philippians 4:6).

Prayer by the Square Spinner

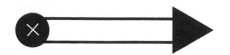

PRAYER BY THE SQUARE

Spin the arrow, and follow the instructions for moving forward or back. If you land on a Bible verse, read it aloud. If you land on a prayer square, pause and pray. Play and pray as long as you like!

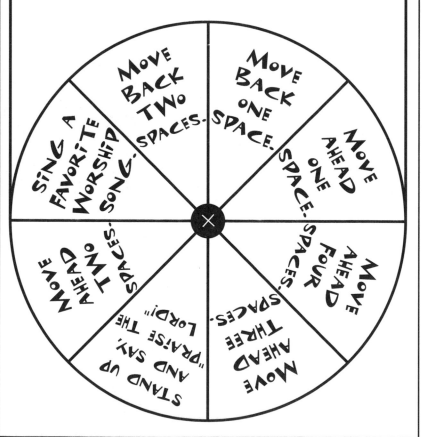

HANDOUT

Hooray! Let's Pray! ● Hooray! Let's Pray! ● Hooray! Let's Pray!

Birthday Blessing Verses

 1. "May the Lord bless you and keep you" (Numbers 6:24).

 2. "May the Lord show you his kindness and have mercy on you" (Numbers 6:25).

 3. "May the Lord watch over you and give you peace" (Numbers 6:26).

 4. "Give your worries to the Lord, and he will take care of you. He will never let good people down" (Psalm 55:22).

 5. "This is my prayer for you: that your love will grow more and more" (Philippians 1:9a).

 6. "That you will have knowledge and understanding with your love" (Philippians 1:9b).

 7. "That you will see the difference between good and bad and will choose the good" (Philippians 1:10a).

 8. "That you will be pure and without wrong for the coming of Christ" (Philippians 1:10b).

 9. "That you will do many good things with the help of Christ to bring glory and praise to God" (Philippians 1:11).

 10. "You are a chosen people, royal priests, a holy nation, a people for God's own possession. You were chosen to tell about the wonderful acts of God, who called you out of darkness into his wonderful light" (1 Peter 2:9).

HANDOUT

Hooray! Let's Pray! ● Hooray! Let's Pray! ● Hooray! Let's Pray!

Birthday Blessings Pocket

Cut out the pocket on the solid lines, and fill in the birthday child's name. Fold on the dotted lines, and use tape or a glue stick to secure it.

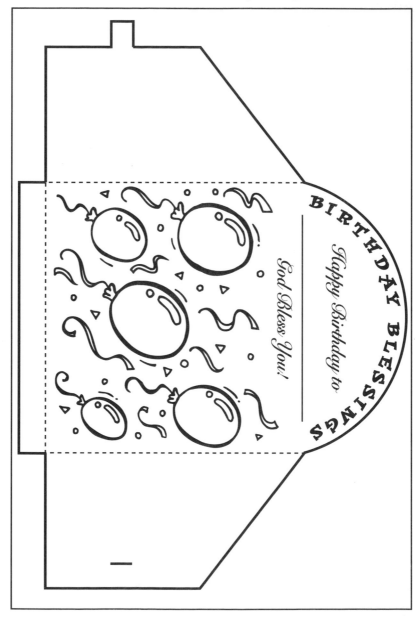

Instant Helps and Handouts

"Anyone who is having troubles should pray. Anyone who is happy should sing praises...Confess your sins to each other and pray for each other so God can heal you. When a believing person prays, great things happen" (James 5:13, 16).

A fourth-grade girl spent a tearful evening because she had forgotten a book that she needed to finish a report due the next day. At bedtime her parents prayed that God would help her reconcile the problem. Stomach flu hit in the middle of the night. Catching her breath after a bout of vomiting, she looked up and announced, "God certainly had a creative solution to my report problem!"

Transform your classroom into an exciting place where kids will *want* to pray! This chapter is chock-full of ideas with prayer appeal, from interactive bulletin boards to a special "prayer closet" where kids can go to be alone with God. Use the prayer partner packets (p. 89) to link kids with senior adults in your congregation.

MAKE ROOM FOR PRAYER
Truth: It's good to have a special place to pray.

In Matthew 6:6, Jesus instructs us to pray in private. Have kids help you transform a corner of your classroom into a private place for prayer. Move tables, chairs, and desks from that corner of the room. Hang a sheet across the corner diagonally. Place a soft throw rug or carpet square on the floor. Set up a small table with a Bible, a small lamp, and a cassette

CHAPTER EIGHT

Hooray! Let's Pray! ● Hooray! Let's Pray! ● Hooray! Let's Pray!

player with tapes of worshipful instrumental music.

Put up a "Welcome to Our Prayer Corner" sign outside your corner. Have kids make posters of important verses about prayer, such as Matthew 5:44 and 6:6; Luke 18:7; 1 Thessalonians 5:17; and James 5:13. Help them hang the posters on the walls.

Let kids help decide how they'll use the prayer corner. They may want to set aside time each week for kids to take turns praying alone inside the prayer corner. Or kids might simply want to use the corner whenever they feel the need. Pairs of children might visit the corner together to pray for each other. Vary the way you use the prayer corner to keep it a vital part of your classroom.

Encourage kids to treat the prayer corner with respect and to be quiet when someone is praying there.

◎ PRAYER COLLECTION

Truth: It's good to ask others for prayer requests.

Have kids "collect" prayers from members of your church. Equip them with a tape recorder and a blank tape. Encourage them to ask questions such as "Is there a special prayer concern you'd like our class to pray about?" or "How can our class pray for you?" When kids return from their interviews, listen to the tapes. Have kids take turns praying for the people they interviewed.

Extra Idea! Have kids send Prayer-grams (p. 92) to the people they interviewed and prayed for.

◎ PRAYER AND CARE PACKAGES

Truth: It's good to pray for others on a regular basis.

As a class project, help kids choose someone they'd like to "adopt" through prayer. He or she might be a missionary, an elderly church member who can't get to church often, someone who's suffering from a long-term illness, or someone in the military.

Create a list of items your "adoptee" might appreciate. You might include a photo of your class, a Bible or devotional book, a cassette or CD of Christian music, a roll of stamps, or a box of stationery. Let kids decide how to raise money to purchase the items and send

CHAPTER EIGHT

Hooray! Let's Pray! ● Hooray! Let's Pray! ● Hooray! Let's Pray!

the package. Be sure to include a letter that tells the person your class is praying for him or her. Have everyone sign the letter.

Continue to pray for the person over a period of weeks or months. Be sure to share any return correspondence.

PRAYER-GRAMS

Truth: It's good to tell others that we've prayed for them.

Use this activity to help your children get in the habit of praying for others. Photocopy the Prayer-grams (p. 92) onto colorful paper. Set out pens or fine-point markers and the Prayer-grams. Each week, have children choose people in the church, community, or government to pray for. Set aside a few minutes in class for children to pray for the people they've chosen.

Then have children fill out Prayer-grams to send to the people they prayed for. If you're working with very young children, fill out the Prayer-grams yourself, and have the children color them. Mail the Prayer-grams on your way home from church.

PRAYER POWER FOR ALL TO SEE!

Truth: It's good to remember God's answers to our prayers.

Help make answered prayers real to your kids with these visual reminders for your classroom.

● **Prayer Chain.** Set out a supply of six-by-one-inch construction paper strips in two colors, fine-point markers or pens, and transparent tape. Designate one color of paper strips to represent prayer requests, and the other color to represent answered prayers.

Encourage each child to write a prayer request or a brief description of an answered prayer on a paper slip of the appropriate color. Then have kids loop and tape the paper slips together (with the writing on the outside)

CHAPTER EIGHT

Hooray! Let's Pray! ● Hooray! Let's Pray! ● Hooray! Let's Pray!

to make a prayer chain. Tell kids that colors don't have to alternate in this paper chain. Hang the chain from a corner of your ceiling.

Each week, allow time for kids to add to the prayer chain. As the chain grows, festoon it around the room. Soon your class will be surrounded with evidence of God's love and care!

● **Prayer Clothesline.** Have kids help you hang two string "clotheslines" in your room. Tape the strings from wall to wall in two corners of your room, or along two flat walls. For extra fun, have kids make paper trees to hang the clotheslines from. Help them twist paper grocery sacks into trunks and attach leaves torn from green construction paper.

Let kids make one sign for each clothesline. The prayer request sign might say, "Left hanging out to dry?" or "Feel like you've been through the wringer?" The answered prayer sign might read, "Worries washed away," or "Just like new."

Provide containers of small hinge clothespins and pens or markers near each clothesline. Photocopy the "Worries Washed Away" handout (p. 93) onto colored construction paper. Enlarge the clothes patterns if you'd like. Have kids cut out the paper clothes outlines. Put the paper clothes in a basket near the prayer request clothesline.

Each week, invite kids to write their prayer requests on the paper clothes and hang them on the request line. When prayers are answered, have them move the clothes over to the answered prayer clothesline. Remind kids that God will "wash away" all our worries when we go to him in prayer.

● **Prayer Poster.** Use markers and a large sheet of newsprint to create a prayer poster for your wall. Divide the poster in half vertically. Invite kids to decorate the poster and to write prayer requests on the left side.

Explain that when a prayer is answered, kids can circle the request, draw an arrow from the circle to the answer side, and write how the

CHAPTER EIGHT

Hooray! Let's Pray! ● Hooray! Let's Pray! ● Hooray! Let's Pray!

prayer was answered. Let this be an ongoing process. Plan to meet in front of the prayer poster each week to pray for requests and offer praises for answers. Remind children that God may answer prayers in several ways. Help children see that even a "no" is an answer to prayer.

PRAYER PARTNER PACKETS

Truth: It's good to pray with a friend.

Consider using this idea to match kids and adults in your congregation as prayer partners. This can be a terrific ministry to kids who are dropped off at your church door and don't have adults at home supporting their growing prayer lives. It can be equally important to seniors in your congregation who feel unattached and unneeded.

Talk with your pastor about what group of adults would be the best prayer partners for your kids. It might be a Sunday school class, a Bible study group, or individuals who have a love for children. Ask adults to make a two-month commitment to write a note every other week.

Photocopy the "Meet Your Prayer Partner!" and the "Prayer Postcard" handouts (pp. 94-95). Give each child two five-by-seven manila envelopes. Have kids each write his or her name on one envelope.

Post these envelopes on the wall outside your classroom or in another convenient location. You may want to take instant-print pictures of your kids to attach to the envelopes.

Have the children each write their prayer partner's name on the other envelope. Have the children fill out the "Meet Your Prayer Partner" page and place it inside the envelope along with several copies of the "Prayer Postcard" page.

Deliver the prayer partner packets to the adult partners. Encourage adults to write a brief note on a Prayer Postcard and place it in their children's mail envelopes every other week. The note could be as simple as "Thinking of you!" or "God loves you." The postcard also includes space for the adult to request prayer for a particular need or problem. Monitor the mail envelopes to make sure that each child receives a response as planned. Add responses of your own to envelopes that may not have received one.

After two months, decide whether you want to continue with the same partners or find new ones. Keeping the same partners helps establish important long-term relationships. On the other hand, meeting new partners helps build more adult-child friendships.

Extra Idea! Kick off your prayer partner program by having kids prepare party foods for their adult partners. Invite the adults to enjoy an informal get-to-know-you party where they can meet and chat with their young partners.

INTERACTIVE BULLETIN BOARDS

Truth: It's good to have visual reminders of prayers.

Bulletin boards can be powerful teaching tools because they're visible to children all during class time. If kids help design the bulletin board, the message will be even more meaningful. Use these interactive prayer bulletin board ideas to jazz up the walls of your classroom and get your kids excited about prayer.

● **Prayer Garden.** Children can add to this bulletin board each week. Cover the bulletin board with a plain background of pale blue or yellow paper. Have kids design, make, and staple paper pots to the board Use the illustration as a guide. Kids could also make pots from colored paper plate halves or tin cans with lids removed. (If you use cans, make sure there are no rough edges that could cause cuts. Flatten one side of each can and use duct tape to attach the cans to the board.)

Have kids use green yarn or chenille wire to turn the pots into hanging baskets. Let them make leaves and flowers from colored construction paper. Each week, have kids write prayer requests and descriptions of answered prayers on new flowers and leaves and then attach them to the board. Soon you'll have a garden growing with God's grace and love!

● **Patchwork Prayers.** Turn your bulletin board into a patchwork quilt of prayers. Before class, cut scrap fabric into three-by-three-inch squares. Have kids use markers to write on the fabric squares names or words that remind them of prayer needs, or of times God answered their prayers. One child might write "chicken pox" to ask God to heal his little brother. Another child might write

CHAPTER EIGHT

Hooray! Let's Pray! ● Hooray! Let's Pray! ● Hooray! Let's Pray!

"Spikey" to remind her of when God helped her find the family's lost dog. Younger kids may prefer to draw pictures on their squares.

Help kids staple the squares to the bulletin board in a patchwork design. You may want to stuff the squares with a bit of cotton or batting to give the quilt a puffy effect.

Tell kids that just as a quilt keeps them feeling warm and secure, praying to God can keep them warm and secure because God loves them, watches over them, and answers their prayers.

PRAYER JOURNAL

Truth: It's good to write down our prayers.

Keeping a prayer journal can be a valuable experience for a child that just may spark a lifelong dialogue with God. In a journal, a child can learn to articulate his or her thoughts, fears, questions, and praises. As the journal progresses, kids can look back and see how God answered their requests, calmed their fears, and helped them learn more about him.

Photocopy on colorful paper the simple prayer journal, "My Time Alone With God" (p. 96). Hand out the journals, and have kids fill in their names and then fold the journals into a booklet. Walk kids through each page of the journal. Explain that the prayer checklist helps us make sure that we're praying the way the Bible tells us to pray. Encourage kids to enter their prayer concerns and praises on the appropriate pages.

You may want to keep a supply of journals on hand, printed in different colors. Encourage kids to pick up new journals when they've filled their first ones.

HANDOUT

Hooray! Let's Pray! ● Hooray! Let's Pray! ● Hooray! Let's Pray!

Prayer-gram

Dear _____,
I prayed for you today. I know God hears and answers our prayers.
Love,

_____

"Do not worry about anything, but pray and ask God for everything you need, always giving thanks" (Philippians 4:6).

Prayer-gram

Dear _____,
I prayed for you today. I know God hears and answers our prayers.
Love,

_____

"Do not worry about anything, but pray and ask God for everything you need, always giving thanks" (Philippians 4:6).

HANDOUT

Hooray! Let's Pray! ● Hooray! Let's Pray! ● Hooray! Let's Pray!

Worries Washed Away

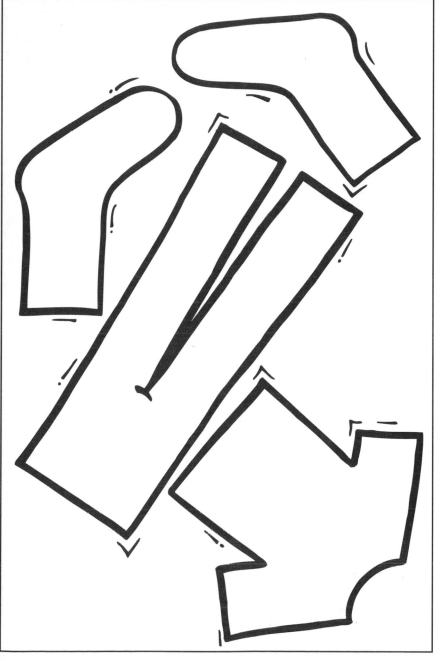

HANDOUT

Hooray! Let's Pray! ● Hooray! Let's Pray! ● Hooray! Let's Pray!

MEET YOUR PRAYER PARTNER!

Name _____

Age _____ Grade _____

Number of brothers and sisters _____

Favorite school subject _____

Favorite sport _____

Hobbies _____

Prayer Requests _____

Please pray for me because: _____

THANKS!

(name)